Career Launcher

Professional Sports Organizations

Career Launcher series

Advertising and Public Relations
Computers and Programming
Education
Energy
Fashion
Film
Finance
Food Services
Hospitality
Internet
Health Care Management
Health Care Providers
Law
Law Enforcement and Public Safety
Manufacturing
Nonprofit Organizations
Performing Arts
Professional Sports Organizations
Real Estate
Recording Industry
Television
Video Games

Career Launcher

Professional Sports Organizations

Christian Schulz

Ferguson's
An Infobase Learning Company

Career Launcher: **Professional Sports Organizations**

Ferguson
An imprint of Infobase Learning
132 West 31st Street
New York NY 10001

Library of Congress Cataloging-in-Publication Data

Schulz, Christian (Christian Dahl)
    Professional sports organizations / by Christian Schulz.
        p. cm—(Career launcher)
    Includes bibliographical references and index.
    ISBN 978-0-8160-7964-3 (hardcover)—
1. Professional sports—Vocational guidance—
United States—Juvenile literature. I. Title.
    GV734.3.S38 2011
    796.0440237—dc23

                                                        2011039164

Ferguson's books are available at special discounts when purchased in bulk quantities for businesses, associations, institutions, or sales promotions. Please call our Special Sales Department in New York at (212) 967-8800 or (800) 322-8755.

You can find Ferguson's on the World Wide Web at
http://www.infobasepublishing.com

Produced by Print Matters, Inc.
Text design by A Good Thing, Inc.
Cover design by Takeshi Takahashi
Cover printed by Yurchak Printing, Landisville, PA
Book printed and bound by Yurchak Printing, Landisville, PA
Date printed: February 2012

Printed in the United States of America

10 9 8 7 6 5 4 3 2 1

This book is printed on acid-free paper.

Contents

Foreword

So, you want a long, illustrious career in professional sports? And you bought this book looking for some helpful tips? Here's one: being a fan is not enough.

Professional sports is big business and in order to get ahead in it, you have to be skillful, proficient, and land the right opportunities. After 18 years at Major League Baseball, I have a few thoughts on the subject I hope you will find helpful.

I first joined Major League Baseball in January 1994 with a job at what was then The Baseball Network. I parlayed that into a similar role in the Broadcasting Department of the Office of the Commissioner. In 2008, I was fortunate to join the team launching The MLB Network, and have now returned to the Commissioner's Office. Having always been involved in the broadcasting side of our business, I remain fascinated by the technology, advancements, and possibilities of the television/radio medium. My role has me working with our network partners (e.g.: ESPN, FOX, TBS), business/content partners (e.g.: DirecTV, inDemand, SiriusXM), each of the MLB Teams, as well as the other major sports leagues and industry groups.

When I was asked to write this foreword, I thought long and hard about the most important keys to success, and I kept coming back to just two: *networking* and *hard work*. You could argue that these two are much like the age-old "which-came-first-the-chicken-or-the-egg?" debate. But the truth is that they are both essential and work very much together.

While luck and timing always play a part, who you know and what you can deliver are key. Respect must be earned; the sooner you realize this the better. Put in your time, ask questions, be diligent, and do anything and everything to get the job done as best as you can. This will earn you the respect of your colleagues, superiors, and other business associates. Earning that respect will open new networking opportunities to help you rise through the ranks. Of course, knowing a few folks in the industry right off the bat can help you get a foot in the door. But as you move up, you will see that both networking and hard work continue to be important. They are the cornerstones of every long and successful career in the sports industry.

So, what's the best way to network? For starters, join every professional or industry group, volunteer, attend seminars, and engage in active discussions with colleagues. Over time you will identify a few contacts with whom you click and who might be in a position to help you, even if not right away; then you keep in touch. Keep in touch with as many people as you can, focusing more on those who share your aspirations, interests, and/or experiences.

It's not just about impressing people in the business; great connections can sometimes come from the most unlikely of places. You never know when a college professor, first boss, colleague, friend, or even a neighbor may come across the perfect job opportunity or be asked to recommend you. This is when that hard work and earned respect can make all the difference. It did for me, in an unexpected way.

My career in sports began officially when an old boss called to ask me if I might like to work with him again. Really, though, it started years earlier. I first met the man who would become my boss when he moved into the house next door to my childhood home. I was neighborly, helped him out, and eventually even babysat his kids. Sounds silly perhaps, but he knew first-hand that I was hard-working, honest, and reliable, and over the years we kept in touch. When the time came, he was more than willing to provide me with a wonderful reference letter, and then eventually even hired me himself.

While professional sports is a very large industry, many of the same people pop up in different roles. Having worked in the industry for so long, I've enjoyed watching colleagues I started out with move on to bigger and exciting roles all over the sports world. I can now call on these friends for advice, networking opportunities, and for actual business.

Over the years I've had some good interns and great colleagues, and I'm glad that I was someone they felt they could turn to for help or just advice. It's very gratifying to pay it forward.

Opportunities at every level of sports management are, like most other things, more limited today. Because the job market is so competitive, it is more important than ever to build, nurture, and grow a solid list of contacts and maintain your pool of references by proving yourself anew in each job you hold with honest hard work.

You can do it and achieve your goals.

Anything is possible if you just stay focused, get involved, and remain willing to work for it.

—Susanne Hilgefort
SENIOR DIRECTOR, BROADCASTING BUSINESS AFFAIRS
MAJOR LEAGUE BASEBALL-OFFICE OF THE COMMISSIONER

Introduction

The importance of professional sports in contemporary American society cannot be overstated. For many of our fellow citizens, the success or failure of their local professional sports franchise rivals in importance most of the other aspects of their lives. It is not uncommon for people to rearrange their schedules around major sporting events, even going so far as to occasionally prioritize them ahead of professional and familial obligations. To say that some people live or die by the success of their team is, to be fair, an exaggeration. But depending on who you're talking to, it may be only a slight one.

Sports are a common bond shared by a great many Americans, and something for us to lean on times of need. And while professional sports do not decide political races, put food in our bellies, or help to pay the rent, they do provide a unifying influence within the world's most diverse country. Fans and players alike will come together in pursuit of the common goal of victory, regardless of their race or culture or socioeconomic background. Sports are no mere distraction from the harsh realities of life in our turbulent society. Rather, they serve as a model of those qualities which are necessary to succeed in America.

Given the passionate public interest and support that the industry enjoys, it is not surprising that professional sports makes for a stimulating and rewarding field in which to pursue a career. The professional sports industry has evolved over time into a multi-billion dollar business. As such, it requires a large number of skilled professionals working in various capacities to feed the public's ever-increasing appetite for athletic entertainment. And unlike pitchers and quarterbacks and point guards and goalies, these front office jobs do not require a stitch of innate athletic talent. These jobs are available to anyone with a solid education, a strong work ethic, and a willingness to work with others in a team environment.

Now that you have chosen to pursue a career in sports, it is in your best interest to familiarize yourself as much as possible with the industry as a whole, its various subdivisions, and the specific careers one can pursue within each of them. It further behooves anyone looking to move up through the ranks to be knowledgeable as to the history, trends, and vocabulary that distinguish the sports industry from all others. *Career Launchers: Professional Sports Organizations* will supply you with everything you need to know in order to think, talk, and conduct yourself like a seasoned veteran from your very first day on the job.

The professional sports industry is made up of a broad spectrum of diverse occupations offering ample opportunity for rapid advancement as well as lateral movement. This book focuses on front office jobs with sports franchises and sports leagues as well as those at sports facilities such as stadiums and arenas. Not included in this book are actual, on-field positions such as coaches and managers. These jobs are generally filled by former players and/or individuals who had some familial connection which afforded them access to this insular world from a young age. (Let's face it, nobody ever landed a job coaching the New England Patriots after buying a "how-to" book.) The professions detailed in this book therefore focus on the three major sources of employment within the professional sports industry—franchises, leagues, and facilities. These professions are myriad and varied, including (but not limited to) opportunities in management, operations, marketing, promotions, sponsorship sales, business development, public relations, ticket/suite sales, accounting, legal services, technology, and security.

The professional sports industry offers copious opportunities for advancement. Through perseverance and willpower, it is possible for an employee who starts out at the lowest levels to rise to the very top. (NFL Commissioner Roger Goodell, for example, began his career as an administrative intern in the league office). Through hard work, study, and erudition, you too can pursue a long and rewarding career path in this challenging and exciting field.

How to Use This Book

The purpose of this book is to help you make the most of your career in the professional sports industry. In the following six chapters, you will be presented with a comprehensive overview of the industry as well as various techniques designed to help you ascend the ladder of success. You can peruse all six chapters to gain a comprehensive view, or simply skip to a chapter of particular interest to find detailed analyses of specific topics. Based on market share, audience size, and amount of jobs available, football, baseball, basketball, and hockey are the central focuses of this book. Other professional sports leagues function in much the same way as the "big four," so information gleaned can be easily transferred if one is interested in pursuing opportunities with, for instance, the Professional Golf Association (PGA) or the International Tennis Federation (ITF).

Chapter 1 traces the origins of the four major American sports as well as their evolution over time. Professional sports leagues and their member franchises have been around since the 1800s, and their sophistication has grown in lock step with their increasing value. A comprehensive understanding of the nature of this growth is of paramount importance to anyone looking to find employment in this industry and/or looking to move within it. This section provides that historical overview. It also includes a timeline that includes major evolutionary events in the sports world as well as pertinent external events that influenced the sports world.

Chapter 2 offers a numbers-driven overview of the sports industry's current state of affairs. This section offers statistics on employment, wages, profits, current and possible future trends, technology, key conferences and industry events, major players and industry forces, and issues of law and government regulation. Since sports play such a prominent and public role in American culture, the leagues and franchises are typically subject to greater government and media scrutiny than other industries. It is therefore incumbent on team personnel to be cognizant of the laws and statutes which pertain to their particular role in the operation.

Chapter 3 describes in detail the various jobs within the professional sports industry. The jobs in this field are numerous and varied. And much like the teams themselves, employees must work harmoniously and efficiently with their co-workers in order to maintain operational efficiency. The sheer complexity of a league or franchise's organizational structure is largely unknown to the general public. For example, the New York Yankees employ 42 people in executive and senior administrative positions alone, with job titles ranging from managing general partner to director of stadium tours. And they are, of course, supported by hundreds of employees in various supporting roles. This professional hierarchy, with its coordinated individual responsibilities, has evolved through trial and error into a system of professionalism which mirrors that of the team on the field. Chapter 3 details the chain of command typically utilized by franchises and leagues to ensure the smoothest possible operation. It also presents potential routes for advancement by detailing the chain of command which exists between the various positions.

In chapter 4, you will find a roadmap for success within each of the sports industry's individual professions, as well as more general advice that can be applied to most any professional endeavor. This includes subsections focusing on job training and continuing education, job search strategies, interview dos and don'ts, as well as tips for successful interaction with bosses and co-workers. The sports industry is comprised of many interrelated professions, and experience in one can often be applied to another. The blueprint chapter 4 provides will help you to familiarize yourself with the industry's structure in order to formulate a gameplan to move between and among these overlapping strata.

Chapter 5 provides a glossary of terms that will help you to successfully communicate with your coworkers. As with most industries, professional sports organizations have developed a distinct vocabulary to describe those aspects which are specific to it. From terms which are specific to the game play of the various sports themselves, to the business terminology which has evolved to distinguish those elements which are unique to the sporting world, there are many words and phrases in day-to-day use that are largely exclusive to the sports industry.

Chapter 6 presents a detailed list of associations, books, and Web sites that offer useful insights about the sports industry and the day-to-day realities of working for a sports league or franchise.

Within each individual chapter, you will find the following boxed features, included to enhance your understanding of a particular topic:

→ **Best Practice:** These tips will help you to enhance your efficiency and performance in the workplace. Though most are specifically aimed at the sports industry, others are more all-purpose tips for professional success in general.

→ **Everyone Knows:** These boxed features detail helpful facts of which everyone in the professional sports industry should be cognizant.

→ **Fast Facts:** These fascinating and useful facts can augment your understanding of the sports field as a whole. They also provide an opportunity to impress your bosses and co-workers with your erudition.

→ **Keeping In Touch:** These features offer tips for effective business communication—whether via e-mail, over the phone, or in person.

➡ **On the Cutting Edge:** These boxes detail emerging trends within the industry. Focusing on the latest trends and advances, these will prove particularly valuable to those contemplating a move to new positions within the sports industry.

➡ **Problem Solving:** These features present case-study-style descriptions of a particular industry dilemma or a hypothetical predicament and a potential resolution, with particular emphasis paid to how a thorough knowledge of the job and preparedness can mean the difference between success and failure.

➡ **Professional Ethics:** Regardless of industry, ethics are fundamental to successful career growth. These boxes detail potential ethical challenges you may face during your career in the sports industry.

Regardless of your educational background or prior work experience, the possibilities for employment and growth within the sports industry are practically boundless. This book will help you to familiarize yourself with the industry as a whole, give you a leg up on the competition, and help to navigate your career path by detailing the information needed to achieve the highest possible level of success within the professional sports industry.

Chapter 1

Industry History

Sports are a cornerstone of American society. American professional teams, in particular, enjoy significant notoriety and celebrity status within our culture. Sports are also linked to values that American society holds dear: integrity, equality, and justice. And they provide a common bond in the form of rooting interest for communities which might be otherwise divided along racial or class line. Sports teams give communities hope in times of crises and happiness in times of hardship. It can be stated without exaggeration that sports teams are as invaluable as other social institutions such churches, community centers, and other social organizations.

American forefathers like Benjamin Franklin and President Thomas Jefferson reiterated and promoted the need for exercise. Dwight Eisenhower, Teddy Roosevelt, and John F. Kennedy all encouraged Americans to engage in physical sports. Basketball is a uniquely American sport, while American football developed from soccer and rugby. The first game of ice hockey was played in the United States in 1893. Baseball, "America's National Pastime," is one of the oldest sports in America, originating as a game as early as the 1700s.

While Americans can and do branch off from these "big four" major league sports in both participation and viewership, they consistently remain the most popular. Additionally, their leagues provide the most jobs for those looking to break into the world of professional sports organizations. For these reasons (as well as for the sake of space), they will be the focus of this book. As mentioned in the introduction, the information covered with regards to these sports organizations can be adapted for positions in other leagues: should your interests be with a sport not covered here, know that the business and marketing practices, facilities maintenance operations, ticket sales and management, public relations and sponsorship strategies, and other such tasks are conducted similarly throughout the sporting world.

History of American Football

American football is a descendant of rugby, which was being played in England since before the 1800s. The boundaries of the rugby field were approximately 80 to 100 yards. The ball was a pig's bladder covered with leather and then inflated. It was kicked at a goal that was three feet wide and marked by two sticks on opposing ends. Working-class men from small towns in England were the participants, and they played aggressively.

By 1845 rules for rugby as a sport were established at The Rugby School in England. The sport was now played by prep schools all over the country. One important change to the game was that the ball could be carried. The formalized positions for players were dodger/halfback, quarter keeper, and forward. As prep school boys grew to be men, rugby clubs with 20-man teams became popular all over England.

The British brought rugby football and association football (soccer) to the American colonies. Both association football (soccer) and rugby were adopted as popular sports throughout American universities. American football evolved over time and was played first at the collegiate level before professional teams ever existed.

American college teams were playing association football (soccer) with no standard rules as late as 1863. But by then, the London Football Association had published rules that stated carrying the ball was not allowed in association football or soccer. Rugby and soccer from then on became distinct sports.

The England National Rugby Union codified its rules in 1871. By 1876 American football was being played according to the rules of the rugby union. The Intercollegiate Football Association was founded that same year and adopted the use of an egg-shaped leather ball. The American game changed rapidly to a form of "ball-possession" based football under the tutelage of Walter Camp. Walter Camp is considered the father of American football. He served as an advisor and coach to the Yale Football team in the late 1800s. Major changes to American football included reducing the players on the field to eleven, changing the line of scrimmage and inventing the down and distance rules. Maintaining possession of the ball and advancing downs remained a mainstay of the game. American college coaches like Eddie Cochems and Glenn "Pop" Warner reinvented the game by utilizing the "forward pass" in plays. American football became an institutionalized tradition for many colleges in the early 20th century. Bowl games fostered fierce rivalries between colleges and drew a national audience. American football rapidly grew in popularity among Americans.

Football associations began to form throughout the United States in the late 1800s and early 1900s. A league known as the Pittsburgh Athletic Club was founded in 1891 and was a staunch rival of the Allegheny Athletic Association (formed in 1890). In 1892, William "Pudge" Heffelfinger, a Yale graduate and football player for Walter Camp, was offered a $500 contract to play in a game for the Allegheny Athletic Association against the Pittsburgh Athletic Club. Heffelfinger was offered $250 by the Pittsburgh Athletic Club but felt it wasn't enough money. Heffelfinger scored the only touchdown of the game and helped the Allegheny Association to beat their archrival. This transactional exchange of money is considered to be the first professional football contract. Because the exchange of money for playing sports was considered disreputable, the contract was kept secret for many years.

By 1882, Frederick W. Taylor's theories of scientific management and efficiency widely influenced the game. This led to the creation of the gridiron field that was created with lines every five yards. Eleven players each were required to gain five yards in three downs of possession. Numerical scoring included two points for a touchdown (later increased to six points in 1912), five points for a field goal (later reduced to three points in 1909), and one point for a safety.

By the early 1900s, many states had several leagues or teams formed that played other teams. The Akron Pros, the Canton Bulldogs, Chicago Tigers, Cleveland Indians, and the Rock Island Independents were some of the first original teams to be formed. As the game moved out West, Ohio became the center for football as an established sport. The very first professional football game was played in 1920 between the Columbus Panhandles and the Dayton Triangles in Dayton, Ohio. The American Professional Football Association was founded in 1920 with Jim Thorpe, an accomplished athlete and

Olympian, as the president of the association. In 1922 the Association changed its name to the National Football League and remained the dominant presence in the sport of football even today. The first professional championship game was played in 1919 between the Canton Bulldogs and the Buffalo Prospects. As football grew in popularity across the country many more teams were added. In 1921, the Green Bay Packers were added to the league. The team still has its name today. The Decatur Staleys were sold and in 1922 the team's name was changed to the Chicago Bears, as it remains today.

The 1958 NFL Championship Game is called the "Greatest Game Ever Played." The Baltimore Colts and the New York Giants played the championship game at Yankee Stadium. The game was tied after 60 minutes and became the first NFL game to go into sudden death overtime. The final score was Baltimore Colts 23, New York Giants 17. The game was televised live on NBC television network. The competitive play and excitement of the game, coupled with the fact that it was televised nationally, helped football become one of the most popular sports the United States.

In 1960, the American Football League (AFL) was formed. The 10 teams from the AFL merged with 16 teams from the NFL in 1970. This created two conferences. The total amount of teams grew to 30 in 1993, and then to 32 teams. The league was then divided into eight four-team divisions by 2002.

The Los Angeles Rams became the first team to televise all of its games. As television grew in popularity during the 1950s, more teams signed television contracts. The NFL championship game on December 23, 1951, was the first televised from the East Coast to the West Coast, on the DuMont Network. The first Super Bowl was won by the Green Bay Packers from Wisconsin. Green Bay defeated the Kansas City Chiefs 35-10 on January 15, 1967.

Football continues to grow in popularity and this in turns drives the success of the sport as its fan base continues to expand.

The NFL tried to introduce American Gridiron Football to other countries. The league had supported the creation of NFL Europa, with five German teams and one in the Netherlands. However, the league folded after the 2007 season.

The NFL is trying to create the International Series to further the game of American football overseas. The purpose of the games overseas is to broaden the fan base using American talent. In 2005, the Arizona Cardinals played the San Francisco 49ers in Mexico. In 2007 the Miami Dolphins played the New York Giants in London,

England, and in 2008 the San Diego Chargers played the New Orleans Saints at Wembley Stadium in London, England. In 2009, the New England Patriots played the Tampa Bay Buccaneers in London. NFL's commissioner, Robert Goodell, has openly spoken about the possibility of holding a future Super Bowl in London. National Collegiate Athletics Association (NCAA) Football also plans to begin playing overseas, with the first game slated to be played in Ireland in 2012 between the US Naval Academy and Notre Dame.

History of Baseball

Baseball (America's "national pastime") is one of the few sports that do not use a clock. Fans can enjoy the ballgame without giving a thought to the game running out of time. The teams determine the outcomes of games through strong play or errors or a combination of both. Perhaps baseball evolved in this way because its origins are rooted in the early game of rounders from Ireland or schlagball that came from Germany—games that were created for leisure. Baseball continues this heritage. The fans can still relax and while away hours of enjoyment watching baseball.

Rounders was a game that was played as early as the mid-1400s by the English and Irish. The game had a batter, bowler, and as many as 15 players on two teams. The pitch consisted of a hitting square, four posts, and a bowling square. The bowler bowls the ball in an underarm swing to the batter who hits the ball and runs to the first post. For each post crossed, the batter gains a point. The game never advanced beyond being played in amateur leagues.

Rounders became popular in America when the English and Irish brought it to the early American colonies. Variations of this game were played and were called baseball, town ball or goal ball as early as 1829. Until the late 19th century, "Base" ball continued to be a local, amateur game for children or a recreational distraction for adults.

In 1845, Alexander Cartwright, a bookseller and volunteer fireman in New York City, formed the New York Knickerbockers Base Ball Club and set down bylaws that were to become the rules of the game. In 1846 the Knickerbockers played the New York Baseball Club also known as the New York Nine in Hoboken, New Jersey. The Knickerbockers lost to the New York Nine. The National Association of Baseball Players was organized in 1857 and charged the public admission to games played by the leagues.

Baseball became popular in the New York area around 1855. Local clubs began competing against each other. The National Association of Base Ball Players was formed in 1863. The organization set down rules for the game, some of which included no tryouts and catching a ball fairly meant that a batter was "putout." The National Association of Professional Base Ball Players was formed in 1871. It went defunct in 1875 and was replaced by the National League in 1876.

Changes to the game's equipment and rules of ball release radically changed how baseball was played. In 1887 new changes included pitching overhand. All the rules of baseball were determined by 1893.

Many eastern cities in the United States had baseball teams by 1899-1901. There were two leagues in the late 1800s that competed against each other: the National League and the American League. Each league had eight teams and there were often legal disputes between them regarding player contracts. The team with the most wins after a regular season in each league won the pennant for its league. The pennant winners played each other at the end of the regular season in the World Series.

Colleges were also having intercollegiate baseball games as early as 1857. The first documented game was between Amherst College and Williams College. In a 26-inning game, Amherst defeated Williams 73 to 32.

Baseball was being referred to as the "New York Game" or as "the National Pastime" by 1860. The Cincinnati Red Stockings were an official team by 1869 and was the first professional team to play amateur and semi-pro teams.

By 1901, the Dead Ball Era was in full swing. This was called Dead Ball Era because offensive play by leagues dwindled. Batters were not taking big swings at the ball but were playing a game that relied on hit and runs and stolen bases. This type of baseball game resulted in low scoring games, which fans did not enjoy. Among other problems with the game, the ball itself posed special issues. The baseball used at the time in a game could be used for up to a hundred pitches. This resulted in a ball that unraveled and became soft when hit. Eventually by 1910, a ball with a cork center was introduced. This caused the play to change, as the ball was harder and could be hit further. Today a baseball is only used for an average of six or seven pitches before it is replaced.

World War I brought baseball season to an end on September 2, 1918. After World War I, the game of baseball went through another tremendous change. Babe Ruth ushered in the Live Ball Era. Babe Ruth had an illustrious career starting as a pitcher for the Boston Red Sox in 1914. He changed positions and became a batter in 1918. He hit 29 home runs in 1919, 54 home runs in 1920 and 59 in 1921. He was sold to the Yankees in 1920 and continued to have a brilliant career there until he was traded to the Braves in 1935. He ended his career shortly after.

Many of baseball's star players served in the military during World War II. Players like Ted Williams and Joe DiMaggio served in the Air Force. Over 500 major league baseball players served the United States during World War II.

As with the military, major league baseball still had segregation as well. Negro leagues still existed during the 1940s. Black players were restricted from the major leagues as early as 1880. Brooklyn Dodgers general manager Branch Rickey signed Jackie Robinson, the first black player in the majors, in 1947. Other black players like Willie Mays and Hank Aaron became huge stars in baseball after Robinson. Integration happened so rapidly that by 1955, there were more black players in the major leagues than there were in the Negro Leagues in 1945.

Baseball continued to grow in popularity and was seen as a successful sport as teams (Milwaukee Braves, Los Angeles Dodgers, and San Francisco Giants) moved out to the western part of the United States during the 1950s. By 1961, the two leagues began adding new teams. This era is called expansion period in baseball and lasted into the 1970s.

Many changes came to baseball in the 1970s. Games were widely televised across the country. Other changes were related to new playing surfaces, like artificial turf. Indoor stadiums were being built and some rule changes differed between the National and American League. In 1973 the American League adopted a rule that allowed a designated hitter to bat for a pitcher.

Players and the ball clubs they were hired by often had disputes during this time period. In 1966, the Major League Baseball Players' Association was formed to unite and support ballplayers. This organization became a major supporting force for changes to player contracts and rules. The Association wanted an end to the reserve clause, which stated that a player should only play for one club unless he was released, traded, or retired. Eventually ballplayers were allowed to have "free agent" status. The Players' Association helped raise players' salary levels and secured pensions for them. These benefits did not come without tensions between team owners and players. There were several baseball work stoppages after 1972. The conflict went on for so long during 1994 that the end of the season was canceled along with the World Series that year.

Today, most teams have new stadiums or are in the process of constructing them. The talent is diverse as many players today are from countries such as Japan and the Dominican Republic. One problem that has plagued baseball, the use of steroids, is being given close attention by the baseball commissioner and is being handled appropriately.

Baseball was introduced to Japan in the 1870s by an American professor, Dr. Horace Wilson. It quickly became popular at Japanese universities. Baseball is popular in Cuba and in other parts of the Caribbean. Baseball has spread to the far corners of the world. Scouts are now looking at players in Russia, China, Australia, and soon Africa. Major League Baseball is at its pinnacle of financial success. The possibility remains for total gross revenue of Major League Baseball to surpass the total gross revenue of the National Football League.

According to the 15th annual 2010 Brand Key Sports Loyalty Index, Major League Baseball now rivals the National Football League for having the "most loyal fans." Brand Keys Sports Loyalty Index is a survey that provides loyalty rankings to professional sports teams to help them increase merchandise, broadcast, and ticket revenue.

Baseball grew into a multi-billion dollar industry, a far cry from its beginnings. Baseball is part of the American heritage and national identity and continues to bring pride to Americans.

History of Basketball

Basketball was always essentially a college sport. It was a calculated invention by a physical education teacher named James Naismith. Mr. Naismith taught the game to young men attending the Young Men's Christian Association (YMCA) Training School in 1891. Today, the school is known as Springfield College in Springfield, Massachusetts. He invented the game at the behest of his boss, Dr. Gulick, who asked him to devise a game that could be a form of indoor recreation during the wintertime. Because Naismith had 18 boys in his class, he made two teams of nine players each. A soccer ball was the first ball used and the object of the game was to pass the ball forward until the player threw it into the opposing team's basket. The first hoops were actually peach baskets that were nailed to the walls of the gym. The players threw the ball into the basket, but had to retrieve it by getting up on a ladder. Holes were cut in

Professional
Ethics

Case Study: Play It Safe

Situation: In the marketing department where you work for a professional football team, one of your colleagues approaches you with a piece of "insider" information: management is poised to select an unexpected player with their first pick in the NFL draft. Your colleague, a PR specialist who thrives on feeling like he is a true part of the team, assures you he has this information on good authority. He tells you he is planning to place a bet on the draft and suggests you do the same, saying, "Info like this doesn't come around too often. It's a sure shot to win."

Ethical Problem: There is a fine line between sharing "insider" information and bandying about unsubstantiated gossip. The colleague in question, however, is wrong to be spreading confidential managerial decisions, no matter how he became aware of them. His decision to gamble on the event makes his lack of discretion even more dangerous.

Solution: Simple: Do not be tempted to place the bet. Gambling within the sports industry is looked upon as a grievous offense, not only because of its legal implications but also because it delegitimizes the notion of sportsmanship professional teams are supposed to embody. If fans find out that staff of their favorite teams have been placing bets on the games—or, in this case, the league events—in which those teams are involved, they will look upon the whole organization with distrust. Make it clear to your colleague that you have no interest in this type of information, and do not share what he told you with others. One exception would be to report his actions to a supervisor in confidence, to ensure you are not implicated in anything should evidence of in-house gambling surface in the future.

the bottom of the baskets. (Peach baskets were used until 1906, and subsequently were replaced by metal hoops with backboards).

These students took basketball back to their hometown gyms, taught it to other boys and men, and the game's popularity spread like wildfire. A mere two months after the game was invented, the Central YMCA and the Armory Hill YMCA played met for an official game that tied 2-2.

was formed as an organization to oversee the rules of the game and eligibility of players. In 1910, the association changed its name to the National Collegiate Athletic Association (NCAA).

In 1938, the Metropolitan Basketball Writers Association sponsored the first college basketball tournament. The National Invitation Tournament's sponsors picked six of the best college teams to play for a championship title. The teams that competed in the invitational grew to be over forty teams. In 1939, The NCAA held its first tournament and it mirrored the National Invitation. The best college teams competed to win the National Championship in these tournaments. Some colleges competed in both tournaments. City College of New York (CCNY) won both the NCAA and NIT tournaments in 1950. By the 1960s, the NCAA tournament became the premier collegiate basketball tournament.

By 1897-1898 the game was a popular outdoor pastime played by both men and women. During World War I, American servicemen brought the sport to other countries. The game also spread throughout the world thanks to the efforts of YMCAs. In 1932, the Fédération Internationale de Basketball Amateur (FIBA) was formed. Today, FIBA manages international competition for 212 international basketball federations.

Dr. Naismith's initial purpose for the game was to be a noncontact sport that was played with finesse. However, early basketball play was rough and aggressive. Some YMCA facilities even banned the sport from their gyms because of its excessive roughness. Basketball could be played on dance floors and in social halls, so, in order to protect the fans, wire cages were placed around the court. Players would often get cut or scraped by the wire caging. It was later replaced with rope netting. Basketball players were often called "cagers" in the early years of the game.

A local team in Trenton, New Jersey, wasn't allowed to play at their local YMCA gym so they rented a Masonic Hall and charged admission to cover the cost. Players got $15 each, and the captains got $16 apiece after they paid for the cost of the rent. This is known as the first professional basketball game.

By 1915, many teams like the Original Celtics in New York were hugely popular with fans. Several other teams were emerging as popular among fans, such as the Buffalo Germans, and later on during the 1930s, the New York Renaissance and the Harlem Globetrotters were two other professional teams with star power.

In 1938, a tournament was set up to determine a national collegiate basketball champion. This first tournament was an invitational that was held in Madison Square Garden in 1938. Temple University was the first national champion. The NCAA took over the tournament in 1939 and it came to be known as March Madness.

In 1937, the National Basketball League (NBL) was the first league to be formed. Its purpose was to promote less roughness in the sport and to protect the players from being exploited by teams' owners and is credited with promoting integration of all-white teams. Another league, the Basketball Association of America (BAA), was founded in 1946. Due to poor fan attendance and low scoring games, the BAA was disbanded. In 1949, the BAA and the NBL merged to form the National Basketball Association (NBA).

The first televised basketball game, held at Madison Square Garden, was between Pittsburgh University and Fordham University. The year was 1940. It created a national sensation and forever thrust basketball into the limelight as a beloved American sport.

Pro basketball came into full swing during the 1940s and 1950s. Teams like the Minneapolis Lakers, the Philadelphia Warriors, and the Boston Celtics had large fan bases. The Boston Celtics dominated the NBA from the 1950s to the 1960s. In the 1960s, pro teams helped expand the fan base with huge star athletes like Wilt Chamberlain on the L.A. Lakers. Later, in the 1970s, Kareem Abdul-Jabbar, with his famed "sky hook" shot, helped make the L.A. Lakers the top team of the decade.

Everyone Knows

The Harlem Globetrotters

The Harlem Globetrotters is a basketball team that played exhibition basketball across the country. The team was formed in 1926 by Abe Saperstein. Saperstein chose Harlem as the home base for the Globetrotters because Harlem was known as the nexus of African-American culture during the 1920s. Today the Harlem Globetrotters still plays exhibition games at many events around the country. The team members are famous for their tricks, comedy, and for their incredible skills with the basketball. They are well known for making difficult shots between players, making hard jump shots, and for spinning and balancing the ball on their bodies and fingertips.

In the 1980s team rivalries fueled by the prowess of players like Larry Bird of the Boston Celtics and Earvin "Magic" Johnson of the L.A. Lakers helped grow the sport even more. The late 1980s also welcomed more prominent players like Dennis Rodman and Isaiah Thomas. Michael Jordan helped the Chicago Bulls dominate the NBA during the 1990s.

The future of basketball both pro and college seem to be heading toward expansion. There is talk to expand the NCAA tournament from 65 teams to as many as 96 teams.

Today the NBA commissioner David Stern is hoping to revamp salary caps (no cap for all-star players), institute higher age limits for starting players to be 20 or 21, and hold out for shorter contracts for current players. The NBA's success has led to an increased fan base for intercollegiate basketball. The NBA recruits the colleges' best players. This leads to an increase in the fans that want to see the best players on the pro teams.

History of Ice Hockey

America's history of ice hockey and our participation in the sport are closely tied to our Northern neighbor, Canada. Ice hockey developed first in Canada and then traveled south of the border to the United States. Our two countries remain closely intertwined with the sport; Canadians and Americans play on either American or Canadian teams and staunch rivalries exist between the NHL teams both Canadian and American.

Most historians thought that the British brought the game of hockey to North America. Recent discoveries have shown however that ice hockey is a mixture of Indian lacrosse, Irish hurling, and British field hockey. British soldiers and Irish and Scottish immigrants played early forms of ice hockey (called shinty or shinning) in Canada. Hockey is believed to have come from the French word *hoquet*, meaning a shepherd's stick.

In 1879, at McGill University in Montreal, Canada, students were already playing ice hockey and they defined the rules of the game. By the late 1800s local clubs and leagues were forming all over Canada. Games were being played at Yale University and The Johns Hopkins University in the United States by 1893. The number of players on a team decreased from nine to seven by a chance occurrence. During a game in Montreal, a team showed up with two less players. Both teams played with only seven players and found that they liked having less than nine players on the ice.

That same year, the governor general of Canada donated a trophy to be given to the best hockey team. Lord Stanley of Preston gave the silver bowl with gold inlay to honor the best team every year. The Stanley Cup is the oldest and most prestigious hockey prize. In 1917, the Seattle Metropolitans became the first American team to win the Stanley Cup.

By 1904, five teams from Ontario and the United States formed the International Hockey League. The league lasted for only three seasons. The National Hockey Association was founded in 1909. One major contribution of this organization was the addition of the six-man team. The NHA was folded into the National Hockey League (NHL) in 1918. The National Hockey League, which was actually founded in 1917, had four teams from the United States and Canada. Yet many of the U.S. teams had only Canadian players. The Stanley Cup is the prized trophy that is awarded to the championship team every year. The Toronto Arenas, a newly formed team in 1918 (later becoming the Toronto Maple Leafs in 1927), won the Stanley Cup in the first NHL championship. In 1924, the Boston Bruins was the first U.S. team to join the NHL. The NHL has 30 pro teams today.

After the end of the Second World War in 1945, hockey became popular in the Soviet Union. Russian hockey players would be fierce contenders in the Olympics. They won their first Olympic gold medal in 1956, only 10 years after ice hockey became an organized sport in the Soviet Union. The 1980 Olympics drew a large audience for ice hockey. The American team, comprised of all amateurs at the time, was pitted against a very strong Soviet team. Because of the Cold War, the American team and the Russian team were seen as natural rivals. It was a huge upset for the Soviets when the Americans won the final game in a dramatic tiebreaker (4-3). This led to the gold medal win for the American team. It is considered one of the greatest moments in sports history.

Women's hockey has been a thriving sport since 1889 in Ottawa, Canada. The women's game saw a decline in the 1960s but it experienced a revival in the 1980s. The NCAA allowed women's hockey to be added as a college sport in 1993. The women's U.S. hockey team won its first gold at the Olympics in 1998. It was the first year the women's team played in the Olympics.

The Zamboni machine was first used to clean the ice at NHL games in 1955. It debuted at a Montreal-Toronto game. To this day the NHL only uses Zamboni machines. A family-owned business, the Zamboni firm operates out of California and now has operations in Canada and Switzerland. The Zamboni machine has became one

On the Cutting
Edge

Losing Trax

In order to make hockey more accessible to American fans, Fox Network decided to create the FoxTrax puck. The puck was fitted with a circuit board chip that allowed Fox to track the puck on TV by showing it as lighted on the screen. There was an outcry from diehard hockey fans to lose the FoxTrax puck because it distracted from the game and the players. Mostly, they argued that anyone should be able to see the contrast of the puck on the ice.

of the entertainment pieces at hockey games, especially for kids. Many enjoy a ride on it as it cleans the ice.

Hockey as a sport always enjoyed some sort of public attention. Scores were being sent over the telegraph from as early as the 1890s. Game descriptions were sent along the wire. The 1896 Stanley Cup was telegraphed out from lines set up at the Montreal Rink. Radio stations in Canada were broadcasting games as early as 1923. The Canadian Broadcasting Corporation (CBC) began televising hockey in Canada in 1952. The first televised game was between the Detroit Red Wings and the Montreal Canadiens at the Montreal Forum. *Hockey Night in Canada*, or *HNIC*, is CBC's most highly rated show and brings in a lot of revenue for the network. CBS was the American network to initially carry NHL games. Hockey was less popular on American television than games broadcasted for the NFL, NBA, or MLB. CBS and NBC were the primary networks that held rights for NHL games, but neither network carried a full schedule and only featured a select few games of the Stanley Cup Finals.

Television has created an infusion of revenue into the league, which has allowed pro teams to pay higher salaries for players. TV has also forced the game to change. NHL rules now require four commercial breaks per period. It gives players time to recover and allows them longer playing time. Neither network carried exclusive coverage of hockey for a 24-year period (1971–1995).

USA Network began carrying a full schedule of games in 1981. ESPN won the contract in 1986 and SportsChannel won it in 1989. ESPN regained the national hockey contract in 1993, joined by the

Fox network in 1995. ABC outbid Fox for the contract in 1999. NBC, and ESPN continue to bid against each other every few years, but the full schedule of games is always carried.

The NHL has had its share of problems. In 2005, the season was cancelled due to labor disputes between the players' union and the league. Play was resumed in October of the same year after an agreement was reached in July.

The promotion of hockey as a sport has come in many ways: CBC, the Canadian network, has premiered movies based on real games and reality shows based on hockey to create interest in the sport. Hockey continues to enjoy a measure of popularity in the United States largely due to games being broadcast on major media outlets and via the Internet, the Olympic Games, and the influx of talented Russian and Eastern European players after the fall of the Soviet Union.

A Brief Chronology

1700: Baseball is being played as a mixture of rounders and schlag ball.

1845: Alexander Cartwright, head of the Knickerbocker Base Ball Club, devises rules for baseball.

1850: California enters the Union as a state.

1861: The Civil War starts.

1869: The Cincinnati Red Stockings is the first pro team in baseball.

1876: American football emerges as an official sport at colleges.

1877: Ice hockey is being played in Canada; it moves to the United States shortly after.

1883: Lord Stanley of Preston, Governor General of Canada, donates the Stanley Cup as the highest prize for ice hockey. The first night game for baseball is played in Fort Wayne, Indiana. The Brooklyn Bridge opens.

1889: The first women's hockey game is played in Ottawa.

1891: Basketball is invented by James Naismith. He is a gym teacher at a YMCA Training School.

1892: Ellis Island opens to welcome immigrants from the world over. William "Pudge" Heffelfinger is paid $500 to play football. It is considered the first professional football contract.

1894: Basketballs are designed for the game as opposed to using soccer balls.

1898: The National Basketball League, the first professional league for basketball, is formed. The Spanish-American War starts.

1903: The Wright Brothers take their first airplane flight. Boston Red Sox beat Pittsburgh (5-3) in the first World Series.

1904: Charles W. Follis becomes the first African-American football player by signing a contract with the Shelby Blues.

1912: Fenway Park opens. The Titanic sinks in the Atlantic Ocean.

1917: Four National Hockey Association teams reorganize to form the National Hockey League (NHL). For the first time, an American hockey team, the Seattle Metropolitans, wins the Stanley Cup. The United States enters World War I.

1920: Babe Ruth is sold to the Yankees. Four football teams meet in Canton, Ohio, to form a professional football league. Prohibition begins.

1922: The American Professional Football Association changes its name to the National Football League. It is the most prominent football league in the Untied States.

1923: Yankee Stadium opens for games.

1924: The first NHL game is played in the United States. Boston Bruins defeat the Montreal Maroons.

1929: Rope netting replaces cage netting in basketball to prevent injuries to players.

1935: The first Heisman trophy winner, Jay Berwanger, is selected. He does not join the NFL.

1939: NBC televises the first baseball game on television. The game is between the Reds and the Dodgers. The first football game is televised between the Brooklyn Dodgers and the Philadelphia Eagles.

1941: The United States enters World War II. Many major league players in football and baseball serve in the armed forces.

1945: The Allies win World War II.

1946: The St. Louis Rams move to Los Angeles, the first team to move to the West Coast.

1947: The World Series is televised for the first time. Jackie Robinson plays for the Dodgers, signaling the end of segregated baseball.

1949: The National Basketball League and the American Basketball Association merge to form the National Basketball Association (NBA).

1951: The first NFL Championship is broadcasted on television.

1952: Hockey Night is televised for the first time in Canada.

1955: The Zamboni machine is used for the first time on ice hockey rinks in Canada.

1957: The New York Giants and the Brooklyn Dodgers move to California. Sputnik is launched by the Soviets. NHL games are carried by the CBS Network for the first time.

1958: The NFL Championship, called the "Greatest Game Ever Played," was played between the Baltimore Colts and the New York Giants. The Colts beat the Giants 23-17.

1966: Football is declared more popular than baseball, according to American surveys.

1967: The first Super Bowl is played as the championship game between the Green Bay Packers and the Kansas City Chiefs.

1974: Hank Aaron breaks Babe Ruth's home run record. President Nixon resigns.

1980: The United States Olympic Hockey Team defeats the Soviet Union and goes on to win the gold medal. The game is known as the Miracle on Ice.

1989: Pete Rose is banned for gambling on baseball.

1994: Baseball players strike. There is no World Series that year. The New York Rangers win the Stanley Cup for the first time since 1940.

2001: On September 11, terrorists crash into the Twin Towers and other sites. It is the first mainland attack on the United States. The Yankees lose the World Series to the Arizona Diamondbacks in November. Yankee wins in New York, however, are a big morale booster after 9/11.

2002: Tsuyoshi Shinjo becomes the first Japanese player to take part in a World Series game.

2004: The United States wins its first ever World Junior Hockey Championship.

2006: The NBA switches to a synthetic basketball that promises improved ball-handling control.

2007: The video replay system becomes a permanent officiating tool for the NFL.

2008: Major League Baseball adds limited instant replay to be in effect for all games.

2011: A jury in San Francisco, California, convicts Barry Bonds of obstruction of justice regarding his use of performance-enhancing drugs. Bonds is sentenced to two years' probation and 30 days' house arrest. The NBA owners' lockout almost ends the 2011–2012 season before owners agree to sharing a larger percentage of sales with players.

Chapter 2

State of the Industry

The four most popular sports in the United States had combined revenue of $23 billion in 2010. Additionally, retail sporting equipment brought in an estimated $41 billion yearly. The total sports market in the United States averages revenue of $400 to $425 billion annually. Other revenue producers include "ticket sales, licensed products, sports video games, collectibles, sporting goods, sports-related advertising, endorsement income, stadium naming fees and facilities income." There isn't parity in terms of games played to revenue earned; for example, the National Football League (NFL) receives eight times more for television and cable broadcast rights than Major League Baseball (MLB). Yet the MLB teams play 10 times more games per season than NFL teams. Team sports revenues are aligned with marketing of the sport and the popularity of the sport. The average NFL team value is $1.04 billion; the average MLB team value is $523 million. National Hockey League (NHL) teams are valued at approximately $228 million per team and the top National Basketball Association (NBA) teams are valued at roughly $369 million. Because the leagues are flourishing, being part of the professional sports industry translates into favorable job outlook and long-term job security.

League Organization

All four major leagues follow a similar system of play each year in which all the teams in the league start at the same point, with no team ranked higher than another because of the performance the year before. Minor league teams or second-tier teams in the leagues do not replace major league teams if they do not have a good season. The opposite actually occurs—the worst teams in football and basketball have the first draft picks of the best players in college. Baseball teams have teams in the AA and AAA leagues. Players can be offered a spot on a professional team if they become good enough. The American sports system is different from the European sports system. The European system allows second tier teams to oust top-division teams based on performance. The American system of team ranking and talent selection allows for the fans to follow a team and players. The American system also allows a team to recruit talent and build a competitive team. The leagues benefit overall because they now get to recruit and retain the best talent in the sport, which fosters more competitive play.

Major League Baseball

Major League Baseball consists of the National League and the American League. The two leagues combined to become one league in 1920. There is one commissioner that oversees the MLB. Twenty-nine baseball teams play across the United States and Toronto, Canada. MLB came very close to making as much revenue as the NFL in the 2010 season. In terms of revenue, it is the second most popular sport in the United States.

Everyone Knows

No Speakers, No-Hitters

Baseball players are among the most superstitious athletes in the world. One well-known shibboleth is the belief that talking about a no-hitter in progress to the pitcher will break the no-hit magic. Even discussion among fans or stadium personnel is taboo, and can result in ostracism of the guilty party.

Baseball is the oldest and one of the most popular sports in America. Baseball has the highest annual attendance of all other professional sports. This is true because the season has 162 regular-season games, more games than any other league plays.

National Basketball Association

The NBA, founded in 1946, now has a fan base that includes countries around the globe. The league has 30 teams across the United States.

The NBA became popular by promoting all-star-level talent. Today the NBA has stars that include players from many countries. Basketball has truly spanned the globe to encompass an international fan base.

National Football League

The NFL has 32 football teams, all in the United States. Although Canada plays its own version of football, there are no American-type football teams there. Football as a sport grosses more revenue worldwide than any other sport, including European soccer, which is played in almost every nation on the planet. In terms of TV ratings and fan base (including stadium attendance) the NFL is the most famous league worldwide. The Super Bowl is the most-watched annual event on television in the United States and internationally, every year.

National Hockey League

The National Hockey League has 30 hockey teams throughout the United States and Canada. The NHL recently expanded to the southern part of the United States. Such teams as the Hartford Whalers from Connecticut moved to North Carolina and became the Carolina Hurricanes. This resulted in a larger fan base that brings more revenue to the sport.

Economic Trends—Present and Future

All top four major leagues remain financially stable. Team wealth and the wealth of all four leagues continue to grow mostly through relocation of teams to other parts of the country. By relocating a team to a different part of the country, the league fosters financial growth and a fan base for the team. Below find some of the current and predicted economic trends for the major sports organizations.

Football

The NFL attendance registered at 66,957 people per game for the 2010 season. Stadium capacity has been at 90 percent for every professional football game played for the last five years. The NFL earned revenues were estimated to be $9 billion during the football season of 2009–2010.

The NFL employs several types of revenue sharing methods. The two main types of revenue sources are retained revenues and shared revenues. Retained revenue is revenue generated and kept by individual teams. This includes 60 percent of gate receipts for home games, local broadcasting rights, sponsorships, gaming rights, concessions, and luxury suites and boxes. Retained revenue was estimated at $3 billion in the 2010–2011 season.

Construction of new stadiums and the sales of naming rights have boosted NFL franchise revenues. This continued trend resulted in 36 arena construction or renovation projects totaling $6.3 billion between 1990 and 2003. Private financing of stadiums' costs is now the preferred method of raising funds to build stadiums. Financing has shifted from 80 percent public funding to 54 percent public funding and 46 percent private funding over the last decade.

Football is big business. Forty percent of the shared revenue comes from national broadcasting rights and fees. Shared revenue in the NFL is also generated from ticket sales at away games and licensing. The total shared revenue for the league amounted to more than $4 billion in the 2010-2011 season. The NFL was part of an eight-year television contract that totaled $17.2 billion, which expired in 2005. Currently networks are paying a combined total of $20.4 billion to broadcast games through 2013.

NFL teams are very valuable commodities. The Houston Texans franchise was purchased for $700 million in 1999. This is a dramatically large increase for the cost of a new NFL franchise. The Tampa Bay Buccaneers and Seattle Seahawks each cost $16 million each when they were new franchises in 1976.

The NFL has been very successful in generating revenue via marketing initiatives. The NFL made $4 billion in sales for the 2000–2001 season. The NFL Properties, which was created in 1963, distributes the revenue that is made with all the NFL team franchises, charities, and the league office. During the 2000 football season, every NFL team franchise received an average of $4 million dollars in revenue. The NFL has had to face stiff competition in more recent years from retailers and vendors in the sporting goods industry who sell football apparel and merchandise at a much lower cost than the NFL.

The NFL has expanded its marketing base to broadband media rights and Internet broadcasting. This trend seems as if it will continue to be a major source of revenue for the NFL. Viacom, America Online, and SportsLine.com, Inc., signed an agreement in 2001 with the NFL worth $110 million dollars over five years. This was an increase over the league's previous contract with ESPN, which was valued at $10 million dollars. The agreement increased the NFL's revenue from $3.3 million annually to over $22 million in the broadcast media market.

The partnerships provided several new broadcast features for the NFL via these new media outlets. AOL provides cross-promotion marketing (online and offline) and interactive services marketing. Viacom aired several NFL productions via the MSG network. SportsLine.com Inc hosted and produced NFL.com, a very popular Web site. SportsLine.com produced the Superbowl.com Web site, which was hugely successful. The NFL Internet Network (NFL.com and the 32 NFL teams) had an average of 16 million visitors per month during the 2010–2011 playing season.

In 2007, the NFL made another mega-TV deal and renewed some prior one-year deals. The NFL and Yahoo! struck an agreement to have a one-year deal for NFL Game Pass (an international service that allows football fans in South America, Australia, Africa, Europe, and Asia to watch games live on the Web). The NFL also partnered with iTunes from Apple for a one-year deal. This service allowed viewers to download videos on NFL Game Day, old Super Bowl highlights, and NFL Replay. The NFL also made another deal with Sling Media to use their video-sharing service. Teams have earned $8.7 million from television deals with CBS, Fox, and ESPN.

The NFL does help generate much revenue from the stadiums that the teams use. The Dallas Cowboys stand at the top of the list as the most valuable team in the NFL, worth $1.6 billion. In 2009 the Dallas Cowboys moved to a new stadium that was slated to bring in $100 million more than the Texas Stadium. Even teams that have lesser values (like the Indianapolis Colts, worth $1.1 billion) are considered very valuable. The Colts have a new stadium, the Lucas Oil Stadium, which will increase revenue by $30 million compared to the RCA Dome.

By 2006, the NFL deals with major television networks (ESPN, NBC, CBS, and Fox) did not cover player expenses. Team owners had to use revenue from box office tickets and luxury suites to pay player salaries. By the end of 2006, the operating income (earnings before interest, taxes, depreciation and amortization) resulted in an average of $24.7 million dollars for each team. This meant the league only made an 11 percent increase in revenue compared to a 21 percent increase from the 2002 season. However, due to large

On the Cutting Edge

Dallas Jumbotron

The Dallas Cowboys erected a Jumbotron screen in their new stadium extending down from the stadium ceiling. It is 25,000 square feet in area, weighs 1.2 million pounds, and cost $40 million to fabricate and install. The Jumbotron was hung too low in the stadium, so punts that are kicked too high hit the big screen. According to NFL rules, these punts have to be re-kicked. Despite the enormity of the screen and the up-close view it affords even the cheapest seats, it has become an example of the hubris for which owner Jerry Jones is becoming increasingly infamous.

sales of sponsorships and high television ratings, the average NFL team is now valued at $1.04 billion, up 4 percent from 2010.

The NFL salary cap continues to be an area of conflict and constant negotiation for players and the league. The cap is a ceiling set by the league for how much a player can earn in a season. These are contracts that are negotiated by the players' agents, the union, and the team owners. The cap is derived from a calculation system, which is based on income that the teams earn during a league year. The revenue was initially limited to defined gross revenues (DGR), which consisted of the money earned from the national television contract, ticket sales, and NFL merchandise sales. Today it includes total revenue such as local advertising and naming rights. In 2006 the salary cap was $94.8 million. In 2009, it rose to $127 million. While this is a complex calculation method that changes yearly, the NFL has been able to manage player salaries while still creating a lucrative deal for valuable players and managing the salary cap much more effectively than other leagues.

Today a pressing issue that the NFL needs to address is the devastating long-term medical effects of head injuries, sometimes carried into advanced age by retired players. Players and agents are calling on the NFL Players Association (NFLPA) to ensure that retired players are taken care of after retirement. In April, the House Judiciary Committee Chairman, Rep. John Conyers, and Rep. Linda Sanchez asked the NFL and the NFLPA to take care of injured players. Both

House Chairman Conyers and Representative Sanchez warned the NFL and the NFLPA they would be subject to attending hearings. These hearings could result in legislation forcing the NFL to put measures in place to support retired or injured players.

Baseball

According to *Forbes* magazine, in 2011, the average worth of a Major League Baseball team is $523 million. Each team averages a net worth of $17.4 million. Despite an economy in recession, all 30 franchises in the MLB posted an operating income (earnings before interest, taxes, depreciation and amortization) of $522 million.

Baseball, as an industry, capitalized on generating revenue beyond just the ballparks as early as the 1800s. Baseball cards with images and player statistics were sold with cigarettes and cigars. The baseball card industry grew and became so popular that older cards are considered to be very valuable and treated as collectibles. Baseball-card sales were at their highest in 1991, when cards brought in $1.2 billion dollars. By 2005, sales decreased to $260 million. Baseball accounts for 45 percent of all sports-card sales—more than hockey, football, and basketball.

When looking at the number of games played in the season, baseball attendance at stadiums is the highest in all the major leagues. This translates into many millions of dollars of revenue. Attendance in baseball has seen a steady increase in recent decades. Attendance rose from 38.7 million in 1977 to 56.9 million in 1991, to 72.5 million in 2004. Local and national television revenues are increasing due to pay-per-view contracts with cable companies, and the use of XM Radio to broadcast games on paid radio.

Baseball has a two-pronged cap system: the luxury tax and revenue sharing. Revenue sharing consists of percenatges of profits like ticket and merchandise sales at stadiums. The luxury tax was put into place after the 2002 agreement was reached between the teams and the league. Teams are taxed if they go above the salary caps. Any team that goes above the cap for the first time is forced to pay a tax penalty of 22.5 percent of the amount they went above the cap. The penalty is higher for repeat offenders. Some teams like the Yankees have paid as much as 40 percent in the luxury tax because of overspending on players. The tax penalty incurred has increased from $117 million in 2003 to $136 million in 2006.

The last big collective bargaining agreement in baseball, in 2003, resulted in moving approximately $1 billion in revenue from the richer teams to the less-revenue rich teams. From 2003 to 2006, it was agreed that all teams would contribute 34 percent of their local revenues to a fund that would be divided equally among teams. Another major change was a central fund set up by a formula that takes $72.2 million from richer teams and distributes it to other, less valuable teams. The fund had a graduated increase to be shared: 60 percent funded in 2003, 80 percent in 2004, and 100 percent in 2005.

The financial outlook for baseball is very promising. Baseball is moving more and more toward catering to wealthier fans, who will pay more for amenities at the ballpark. Baseball still appeals to the average citizen who will turn to watching television or live streaming media on the Internet for games rather than paying for pricey tickets at mega-stadiums with plush amenities.

Player costs in terms of salaries, bonuses, and benefits have been decreasing. Fans are posting huge attendance records, ticket prices are increasing, and the TV rights that come along with the games generate large revenue streams. Baseball teams with less value are doing well because they get to participate in revenue sharing that is capped at $30 million per team.

Fans continue to support their local teams, as is seen in the huge ratings posted on regional sports networks and record attendance at ballparks. For example New York City's Mets and Yankees teams had 8 million fans in attendance while Los Angeles teams had 7.5 million in attendance. However, fans are not willing to watch playoffs and World Series games if their teams are not playing. MLB is turning to the international market to generate more business for playoff games.

In the 2010 season, Major League Baseball expected to make $2.75 billion in revenue from the sales of licensed merchandise. MLB.com, the official Web site of Major League Baseball, was expected to generate over $25 million in auctions and sales of licensed merchandise and collectible items. An additional $9.5 million in revenue was expected to come from online ticket sales. The MLB Web site registers about two million hits a day. Visitors to the site are able to look up detailed information on players and the latest stats on all players. The MLB hopes that visitors who browse the Web site will purchase items from the site as well.

Random drug testing of all players for steroids was instituted as part of the collective bargaining agreement in 2003. In 2004, MLB and the players association added androstenedione to its list of banned substances. The over-the-counter supplement, known as "andro," became a controversial issue when Mark McGwire disclosed he used "andro" during his the season when he hit 70 homers. The Health Policy Advisory Committee (HPAC) is made up of one attorney from MLB, one attorney from the players' union, and a medical representative selected by both sides. The parties must vote unanimously for a drug to be placed on the Major League testing list. Recently, steroid drug use by players has been disclosed and has resulted in several senate hearings in which players appeared before hearing committees. Players are fined or lose game time if it is found that they used steroids that are placed on the MLB list.

A new trend in Major League Baseball is the use of vision-enhancing improvements to the MLB Web site for the visually impaired. An agreement was reached between the MLB, the teams, and the American Council for the Blind where MLB and the teams would make their Web sites accessible to visually impaired fans. The product, called Gameday Audio, would offer volume control, the ability to choose a home or an away feed, and the ability to archive old games.

Basketball

According to the publication *Kagan's Business of Basketball*, the average NBA team was valued at $235 million dollars in 2002, a figure which has risen steadily over the past decade. Basketball has grown in popularity and that in turn has increased the fan base. Fan attendance was recorded at 17 million in 1993. By 2004, over 20 million fans packed basketball venues. Ticket sales were roughly $1 billion at games. Television contracts also drive revenue for the NBA. Expenses such as player salaries, arena revenues, and licensing and ticketing fees are some of the major expenses NBA teams juggle. As with other major league sports, a salary cap in 1999 provided owners the ability to manage and foresee expenses. Local and national TV contracts rose to almost $1 billion in 2001, giving owners more flexibility in paying players and meeting costs. According to the National Sporting Goods Association, basketball fans spent $235 million in 1993 for merchandise and gear. By 2003, fans were spending $300 million dollars on products and other basketball-related items.

As of 2010, according to the *Chicago Tribune*, the NBA told teams at the annual Board of Governors meeting that they can expect a projected 2010–2011 salary cap of $56.1 million. This reflected a $2 to $3 million increase higher than what teams initially expected. This in turn meant that many players would be on the free-agent market, the most ever in NBA history. On average, an NBA coach's salary is expected to cost teams roughly $3.4 million. This figure is lower by 10 percent than in previous years. Any teams' salaries that exceed the salary cap of $56.1 million dollars will be subject to fines on a dollar for dollar tax. The new league salary cap formula used resulted in a decrease in cost for owners of teams while still allowing a 2.5 percent increase in revenue.

The NBA's new collective bargaining agreement with the players calls for player costs to be capped at 57 percent of revenues. If a player's salary were to exceed 57 percent of revenues, then 9 percent of total player costs would be placed back on the owners of teams. During the 2009 season $194 million in overage was reverted back to team owners. This averages out to $6.5 million per team.

The NBA is turning its sites to overseas markets as far as India to further generate revenue for the league. Basketball is now being followed by the younger population in India, which means about 130 million people are watching basketball on Indian networks. American networks are hoping to get a foothold in the media market in India. The NBA also is trying to promote basketball in schools in India. The NBA launched programs called "Basketball without Borders" and "Hoop." In 2008, Robert Parish went to India to teach coaches how to play a better game.

The NBA is also taking "going green" seriously. Many teams are taking on innovative green initiatives. For example, the Phoenix Suns installed solar panels in their arena in an effort to reduce energy use. The L.A. Lakers encourages fans to recycle cell phones that go to local domestic violence shelters. The Dallas Mavericks now holds an e-cycle drive at their arena where fans can bring old computer equipment, cell phones, and other electronic devices and get a chance to win two Mavericks tickets in the playoffs.

The NBA continues to add other initiatives that will generate revenue and save the league unnecessary expenses. The NBA Rookie Transition program offers workshops on everything from networking to gender violence to breaking cycles of drug and/or alcohol abuse.

(continues on page 32)

INTERVIEW

Constant Communication

Lisa Quinn
Director, Events and Attractions Group, NBA Entertainment, Secaucus, NJ

What do you enjoy most about your job?
I enjoy several aspects of my job. I enjoy being able to gain experience in a number of different areas. This has allowed me to be more of a "generalist" as opposed to a "specialist." I think that this helps me to be more marketable within the industry and within my own department, as well as provides me with the opportunity to be able to work on different projects and tasks within the NBA and my department. I also enjoy the fact that my job has taken me to places that I never would have otherwise visited. I have been to China (four times), Singapore, Turkey, and many different cities throughout the United Kingdom. I have seen some things that most people only dream of: the Great Wall of China, the Terra Cotta Warriors in Xian, China, just to name a few. I enjoy seeing and experiencing new places, so the travel has definitely been a high point of my career at the NBA.

Tell me how you entered the field? What was that like?
I technically entered the field while completing my M.B.A. at Robert Morris University. My love for the game of baseball led me to pursue my M.B.A. (with a sports administration concentration) at Robert Morris University (RMU) in Pittsburgh. While finishing up at RMU, I was lucky enough to land an internship with the fan event that took place within the Major League Baseball (MLB) All-Star Week in 1994. From that internship, I ended up working for a Pittsburgh nonprofit organization that produced the first-ever First Night Pittsburgh event. This job came about because of the reputation I earned while working with MLB. After constant communication with the right people at MLB, I landed an entry-level position within the promotional events department. Having grown up a Pittsburgh Pirates fan, getting the job at MLB in New York City was a dream come true to me. After almost five years at MLB, I moved over to the NBA and I have been here for 10 and a half years.

What traits are essential to success in your field?
Hard work, dedication, and networking are all essential to being successful in the sports industry. A good reputation is also imperative. People within the industry talk, and you never know who you will

end up working with and what they may have heard about you. The goal is to be sure that people only have good things to say based on their experience working and interacting with you. A person's hard work and dedication is what will help to formulate a respectable reputation within the industry.

Consistent networking is essential for growth. Knowing your counterparts at other organizations and companies is helpful. Speaking to these contacts on a regular basis is important to keep you up to speed on what else is happening throughout the industry. You never know where that next great idea or your next job opportunity may come from.

When it comes to reputation, what matters most to the sports professional?
Believe it or not, the sports world is smaller than people may think. Having a good, solid reputation is key to succeeding within the industry. There is a lot of movement within the industry. Whether someone moves from league to league, to an agency, or to a sponsor or partner, you really never know who is going to end up where and who you may be working with again. You really want to be well respected amongst your peers and others in the industry.

Are mentors important in the sports industry?
Mentors are important in any industry. Having someone to look up to who can teach you and show you the ropes is a good thing. The world of sports is ever changing and evolving and learning from experts is essential for one's own growth. It is always good practice to have someone to look up to, someone that you want to model yourself after. The key is to align yourself with someone who you respect and who is respected by his or her peers within the industry. With a good mentor, the sky is the limit as to what you can learn.

What role does technology play in your work life?
Communication is key, and without it you cannot guarantee that you will have the information you need to get your work done to the best of your ability. Working at the NBA requires the need to constantly be accessible, whether in the U.S. or in another country. When I first started at the NBA I was handed a cell phone and pager (yes, I really said a pager). This was how we were expected to stay connected. Since then, obviously, technology has come a long way. Now with the help of our company-issued BlackBerrys, we are able to stay connected, regardless as to where we are in the world. I went to Machu Picchu on vacation and my BlackBerry worked! This technology, which allows us to keep on top on information instantaneously, is essential for success in our fast-paced environment.

(continued from page 29)
Hockey

Even though the NHL is the fourth largest North American professional sports league, it has had its most profitable year to date. According to *Forbes* magazine, during 2008–2009, the league averaged an operating profit (earnings before interest, taxes, depreciation, and amortization) of $6.1 million per team. This is the highest figure in the twelve years. The aggregate revenue (including proceeds from non-hockey events at arenas) was $70 million dollars. The 2008–2009 season saw aggregate revenue of $2.82 billion dollars. Today the average NHL franchise is valued at $223 million dollars.

In July 2005, the NHL and the NHLPA managed to put together a player contract that had a salary cap for the first time. That deal with the salary cap has been effective for both the players and the league. The collective bargaining agreement ensures fair salaries to players while still bringing revenues in to the NHL team owners. The salary cap increases each year, starting at $39 million in 2005 to $57 million today. The minimum a team can pay to hockey players in salary is $40 million.

The NHL players' will get 54 percent of the revenues only if the league's revenues are below $2.2 billion. When revenue increases between $2.4 to $2.7 billion, the players will get 56 percent of the revenues and 57 percent when the earnings are over $2.7 billion.

The collective bargaining agreement (for the NHL players) ensures that the players also receive signing bonuses and performance bonuses. In the case of injuries that are long term, players will not receive any of it as per the contract agreement. Team owners can issue a "replacement salary" that doesn't count against the teams total salary payout. When the injured players return to the game, the team must resume following the payroll agreement.

The salary cap ensures that players can't receive more than 20 percent of the team's annual compensation. This includes all the signing, roster, reporting, and performance bonuses, as well as salary. For the 2005–2006 year players were not allowed to make more than $7.8 million; in 2006–2007 the salary was increased by $450,000; in 2007–2008, by an additional $475,000 more; in 2009–2010, by an additional $500,000; and in 2010–2011, players' salaries could possibly increase by $525,000. In 2012–2013 the contract may be extended by the NHLPA. Players who had less than the minimum salary for the 2005–2006 season either had their contracts bought out or were given a mandatory increase to the minimum.

Only under certain types of situations could performance bonuses be given: senior players over the age of 35 who signed one year contracts, entry-level players who are now pro, and players who received one year contracts upon returning from a long-term injury.

Entry-level or draftee players could make $850,000 in 2005, and it would increase by $25,000 thereafter for the next seven years. The signing bonus of a player could not exceed 10 percent of the players' compensation during any year of the contract. Entry-level players or draftees could sign up to $850,000 in performance-based bonuses per year; each bonus could not exceed $212,000. Players could also earn other types of bonuses but could not exceed $2 million in compensation for the year.

Players in the NHL will receive 56.7 percent of hockey-related revenue according to their new collective bargaining agreement. Twelve percent of NHL salaries ($207.6 million) was reverted back to the owners.

New partners that invested in the NHL helped boost the leagues earnings for the 2008–2009 season. Companies like Visa, Energizer, Honda, and CISCO that invested in the NHL helped increase sponsorship revenue and gate receipts to $1.19 billion. This is a 1.5 percent increase from the previous year.

The NHL's largest increase in revenue for last season was from local television. Major markets like Detroit, Toronto, and Chicago signed new contracts that resulted in a $356 million profit. This was a 15 percent increase from the previous season. The NHL's "Original Six" teams are the most valuable franchises to date thanks to the new infusion of sponsorship money.

TV ratings were up by 24 percent in 2009. The NHL also saw an 11 percent increase in the use of the Web by hockey fans. In 2009, the Stanley Cup playoffs were the most watched on TV since the 2002 season. The playoffs generated $80 million dollars in rights and licensing fees for the NHL. The playoffs also generated a large number of visitors to NHL.com. The number of visitors to the site was 12.2 million hits. This was an increase of 33 percent.

The NHL's online marketing product, "GameCenter Live," logged an increase in visitors by 50 percent in 2009. Views of streaming videos the NHL Web site increased 139 percent. Sales revenue from merchandise and other products resulted in a 32 percent increase at the NHL online store. The NHL Store in New York City saw an 11 percent increase in sales from merchandise and collectible items.

The future for the NHL is in generating interest in hockey by starting to expose younger fans to the game all across the United States and Canada. The NHL started a new program in 2010 called "Hockey Is for Everyone." This new initiative supports hockey leagues across the United States and Canada. This nonprofit organization has the support of NHL players, both current and retired, and fans. The program allows boys as well as girls to learn how to play hockey. To date, over 45,000 children have been involved in the program. Additionally, "Hockey Is for Everyone" reaches out to disabled and diverse communities. "Hockey Is for Everyone" celebrated during the month of February. The goal of the program is to continue to promote awareness of the game and generate interest across the United States and Canada with a younger population.

Employment Statistics and Trends

According to the U.S. Bureau of Labor Statistics (BLS), in 2008, 1.5 million Americans were counted as working in the recreation and amusement industry sector. The Bureau of Labor Statistics is predicting that the pro-sports industry will have to be innovative in the way they market their products. Merchandise, ticket packages, and sponsorship sales will have to be marketed to consumers and advertising investors in creative ways that cut costs but also bring in revenue.

The BLS also listed that pro-athletes accounted for 13,960 of that workforce. Other pro-sport jobs included 175,720 coaches and scouts, as well as 12,970 umpires, referees, and officials. Additionally, across the job market, employees in public relations, promotions, advertising, and sales managers occupied 623,800 jobs in 2008. In the fields of advertising, marketing, promotions, public relations, and sales managers, employment is predicted to increase by 13 percent to the year 2018.

The pro-sport teams total about 130 teams for the NFL, MLB, NBA, and NHL. Altogether they grossed annual revenue of $16 billion dollars in 2008. Sixty percent of this revenue is centralized with the top 50 sports franchises. The professional teams' major revenue streams break down as follows: advertising and endorsements, 10 percent; television and radio licensing fees, 40 percent; and ticket sales, 40 percent. The current global recession has affected pro sports. In 2009, professional teams in all four leagues had to struggle to meet the challenge of selling tickets to fill every seat in a stadium or arena.

However, the fans are still fans of their favorite sports and do buy tickets as well as merchandise, but they have cut back in general and have shied away from luxury and big-ticket items. To control expenses, the NFL laid off 150 employees at the end of 2008. Pro-teams will need to meet the challenge of controlling expenses while still bringing quality entertainment to fans. However, despite a tight labor market and expense control challenges, there are still jobs available in the pro-sports industry that need to be filled by qualified candidates. On average, employment is expected to grow at a rapid pace. Managerial positions always have stiff competition but growth within the industries that utilize these positions will be able to absorb the candidates looking for work. Most of the job openings will occur because of the need to replace workers who retire or move into other jobs in the workforce.

Fast Facts

Indy 500-Squared

The largest sports facility in the United States is Indianapolis Motor Speedway. It seats 250,000 people.

Sports venues are generating a lot of revenue for teams and leagues. One hundred and seventy five sports venues have been constructed over the last twenty years, most of them for major sports teams. In the 1990s, $20.4 billion was spent on construction of sports venues compared to only $15 billion spent in the 1980s.

Between 2000 and 2007, nine arenas and 27 major league stadiums were built in the United States. The total cost is estimated at $7.95 billion for constructing the stadiums and $1.97 billion to build the arenas. The average cost per stadium was $215 to $300 million per venue. The expansion of professional and collegiate sporting events accounted for much of the building growth in the 1990s and early 2000s. Cities also vied for teams in order to develop their economic bases.

Premium seating or luxury boxes are big-ticket seats at the stadiums. Premium seating could cost anywhere from $150,000 to $350,000 per season. Club seating and personal (permanent) seat licenses or seats for life are popular sales initiatives that are pitched even before the stadiums or arenas are built. This ensures pre-construction capital will be raised and the projects can be completed in a timely manner.

According to the BLS, marketing managers can expect to see job growth in their field at a 12 percent rate from 2008 to 2018. Sales managers can expect job growth at 15 percent from 2008 to 2018.

The annual median income for advertising and promotion managers in May 2008 was $80,220. Marketing managers earned an average of $108,580, and sales managers saw earnings of $97,260.

People in the marketing field can expect their jobs to change in a way that makes new demands on them. Newspapers, radio, and TV are becoming antiquated ways of reaching the public. Marketing workers must devise new and creative ways to promote goods and services. Public relations managers can expect 13 percent growth from 2008 to 2018. Companies will continue to focus on customer relations that will further develop their popularity with the public.

According to the BLS, advertising and promotions managers will see very little movement in the job market from 2008 to 2018. College graduates with internship experience, creativity, and good communication and computer skills will be able to get these prized jobs. Employers will want to hire candidates who understand the new marketplace and can conceive marketing campaigns involving the Internet and other media sources. In 2008, the median annual wages for advertising and promotions managers was $105,960. Public relations managers made an average of $89,430.

The executive employee working within the professional sports industry can expect to earn approximately $325,000 in salary. Other jobs' compensation varied according to level of education, experience, and skills required to execute the work responsibilities.

Chapter 3

On the Job

The sports industry employs thousands of people in myriad positions. Much like sports teams themselves, the operations within the industry only function properly when the employees at each position accomplish the functions of their jobs with maximum proficiency. From the general manager to the concession salesperson, each team member must perform his or her duties with efficiency and professionalism to ensure the absolute satisfaction of their fan base.

Following are overviews of the various jobs that make up a professional sports organization. The first section discusses sports team jobs, while the second section focuses on sports league positions. The final section offers an overview of the various positions at sports facilities.

Team Jobs

Employees of professional sports teams accomplish a variety of different tasks, ranging from the marketing and branding of the team, to soliciting sponsorships and maintaining business relationships with those sponsors, to selling tickets and suites. Still others work as planners and managers whose logistical responsibilities are integral to the franchise's financial stability. Each professional sports team job section will include an overview of the specific responsibilities for that particular job as well as the training and experience required for an individual seeking employment in that position.

Director of Community/Public Relations

A professional team's value is not based solely on its balance sheet but also, in the larger perspective, by the strength of its relationship with the fans. This relationship is crucial for any team's success. Significant emphasis is therefore placed on maintaining and/or improving the image of the team in the public perspective and building public confidence in general. A team will always benefit from presenting itself as an asset to the community, and doing so helps to offset negative publicity from unforeseen and/or unavoidable problems such as injuries and their sometimes devastating effect on the team's win-loss record.

People who pursue a career in public relations must be skilled in the art of making friends and influencing people. Their primary job function is to influence the media to run stories that present their team in a positive light. PR people must be focused and competitive yet simultaneously able to function as part of a unit. The crucial characteristics required for success in public relations jobs include: creativity, initiative, sound judgment, and excellent communication skills. Quick thinking, problem-solving ability, and highly-developed research skills are also imperative. There are few set standards for entry into the public relations field, but a four-year college degree (typically with a public relations, journalism, advertising, or communications major) in combination with relevant work experience (e.g., media background) is considered excellent preparation for public relations work. Additionally, internships are often extremely helpful for those looking to find employment with a professional team.

Although the majority of PR directors in professional sports do not have them, accreditations are available to those interested in separating themselves from the pack. The two most significant of these are the Universal Accreditation Board, which accredits members of the Public Relations Society of America, and the International Association of Business Communicators (IABC), which offers accreditation to professionals in the communications field, including public relations.

Many teams have entry-level assistant positions in the public relations area (as well as the aforementioned internships), which will afford the recent graduate a rung on the ladder that eventually leads to management-level employment. The BLS has determined that the director of public relations for professional teams could earn from $25,750 to $80,000. Other sports media sources have indicated that the PR director salary could be much higher than listed by the BLS. The following are estimated salaries that can be made in pro sports by an entry-level PR director: MLB could pay $35,000 to $50,000; the NFL, $35,500 to $55,000; the NBA, $30,000 to $50,000; and the NHL, $25,000 to $45,000.

Director of Sponsorships/Partnership Business Development

Sponsorships are a major revenue stream for professional teams in all of the major leagues. Sponsorship is defined as the exchanging of resources between two or more parties that each party deems equal. When a sports team is involved, the exchange is between the team (property) and an outside company whose marketing objectives are met through association with that team. The goals of the sponsorship are different for each side. The team seeks capital investment, media exposure, and reduced prices on products and services. The sponsor company may want a number of things, including increased product awareness, image enhancement, a means to effectively demonstrate products and/or services, and, of course, product sales opportunities.

Directors often rise from the ranks of ticket sales managers and/ or account executives. Directors oversee the sales and account management staff and coordinate strategies for targeting companies for sponsorship. Directors also work with the league office to stay current on open sponsorship opportunities.

It is crucial for directors of sponsorship to develop a complete understanding of sponsorship strategy. Many directors obtain master's degrees in business administration, marketing, sports management, or some combination thereof. The NHL pays a director $50,000 to $80,000; the NBA pays from $60,000 to $90,000. In MLB, a director could make from $60,000 to $105,000; in the NFL, the pay could be $70,000 to $110,000.

Director of Suite Sales

The director of suite sales and services oversees the day-to-day activities of the season's premium seating sales and service department as well as the group sales department. The job requires leadership skills and the ability to develop creative sales strategies, generate new business, train subordinates, implement effective sales practices, and track results. Suite sales directors typically work hand-in-hand with the sponsorship sales and account management teams, because teams often utilize suites to attract partner companies.

As with any director position, the suite sales director must offer guidance to the suite/group sales account executive team, guidance which includes recruiting, training, and development of all staff members. Suite sales directors typically coordinate with ticket sales directors to develop and execute service strategies and promotional plans in order to realize franchise ticket sales goals.

It is incumbent upon anyone in a managerial season ticket and group ticket sales position to implement systems for ticket sales efforts that address the following: sales and service methodologies, lead generation, product development, and the implementation of creative strategies which result in maximizing ticket sales revenue.

Like their general ticket sales director colleagues, suite sales directors are expected to accomplish other related tasks, especially in smaller markets where teams often have a smaller marketing and community relations staff. This includes oversight of customer service inquiries, coordinating timely response to fan requests and feedback, updating senior management and the central accounting office with weekly sales reports, and taking part in related franchise marketing, sales, and event projects.

The director of suite sales can make the following salary ranges in pro-sports. In MLB, he or she could make from $65,000 to $110,000; in the NFL, $70,000 to $120,000; in the NBA, $65,000 to $100,000; and in the NHL, $56,000 to $87,000. Note this position has a wide pay range because it is partly based on commissions.

Director of Ticket Sales

Ticket sales directors ascend to their positions via success as a ticket sales account executive or suite/group sales executive—success garnered through hard work on the front end demonstrating sales aptitude. Although it is not generally a requirement, most ticket sales directors have at least a college degree. Most do not have a graduate degree, but those who do generally have a master's in business administration (often with a focus on sports). The most important characteristic needed to get to the directorial level is success as a salesperson.

The director of ticket sales position is suited to a dynamic professional who is an energetic and creative salesperson with a proven record of success. This position represents one of the key sales roles within the professional sports franchise framework and is tasked with helping the franchise achieve its financial goals while simultaneously maximizing customer satisfaction.

In addition to overseeing the selling of tickets, the director's position typically includes some marketing aspects. Directors sell and market all season, mini-plan, group, and premium ticket packages assigned to them. Besides monitoring, managing, training, and motivating his or her account executive team, this position often requires direct sales via telephone and face-to-face presentations. And because selling is still part of the job, a working knowledge of the franchise's ticketing software is crucial to success in this position.

Best Practice

Varying Job Descriptions

Job titles may differ from team to team. For example, what one team calls the "marketing director" may well have many of the same responsibilities as another team's "vice president in charge of sales and marketing." When researching job opportunities and formulating a career path, be sure to carefully study job descriptions. Don't overlook a position simply because the title seems inconsistent with your chosen path. It may actually be a perfect fit.

Given the increasing importance of Internet marketing, many directors must develop and maintain a database of major corporations, small businesses, and individual prospects via prospecting and networking efforts within the local community.

Other related tasks which may be delegated to the ticket sales director (especially to those with smaller staffs) include monitoring customer service inquiries, implementing and updating systems for responding to fan requests and feedback, creating weekly sales reports for senior management and/or the central accounting office, and taking part in related team marketing, sales, and outside event activities.

The director of ticket sales could make the following salaries at the entry-level: for MLB, pay could range from $65,000 to $100,000; in the NFL, $75,000 to $110,000; in the NBA, $67,000 to $95,000; and in the NHL, $55,000 to $85,000.

General Manager

All professional sports teams have general managers (GMs), who work long, arduous hours trying to build a popular, successful team.

The GM reports directly to the team owner and has the greatest overall responsibility for the franchise's success, as he or she bears the responsibility for supervising all of the day-to-day details of the team's operation. The individual in this position has a lot of power and prestige. If things are going well, the GM receives much of the credit. When things go poorly, the GM is often blamed and, if the slump continues, may well be terminated. Always bear in mind that sports is a multibillion-dollar industry. The qualifications required for a sports administration position are generally the same as those required for any successful business venture. Not surprisingly, the responsibilities of the professional sports team's general manager are similar to those of any individual running a multibillion-dollar business. The GM may work for a major league team or, depending on the structure of the sport, among different levels of minor league teams. The GM's various duties largely depend on the size and importance of his or her specific team. The position's primary function is supervising every aspect of a team's activities. Individuals working with smaller teams or at the minor league level may be personally responsible for the actual day-to-day, operational functions. These duties might include, but are not limited to, oversight of the concessions and hiring the ticket takers, ushers, and additional box office personnel.

To give the organization the best chance for success, a good GM will surround him- or herself with the best team, both on and off the field. The GM, for example, may recommend the hiring of the club secretary, assistant manager, marketing people, publicity people, and trainers. Additionally, he or she is responsible for putting together a winning team. To that end, he or she will usually have a hand in the trading and drafting of team members. It is important that the GM stays current on the activities and background of all of the players in the sport. In collaboration with the owner, the general manager will help decide salaries for team members and support personnel. As athletes become more and more popular (and therefore valuable to the franchise) their salaries increase. It is incumbent on the general manager to put together a team that is popular and, therefore, draws as many fans as possible to their games and other events. Keeping the stadiums filled is tremendously important to the bottom line of professional sports teams. Popularity puts money in the teams' coffers. It means sold-out games and good marketing prospects. It also ensures a strong bargaining position during negotiations of television and radio contracts.

The GM is ultimately responsible for all publicity, press, and marketing of his or her team. General managers of larger, more prestigious major league teams typically hire and supervise the people who accomplish these jobs. The extent to which the GM deals with this area does depend somewhat on the leeway the team owner gives him. The general manager must do everything in his or her power to ensure the team and its organization is operating efficiently. Everything falls under his or her purview, from the ticket takers and ushers to the moneymaking concessions, and he or she must ultimately oversee all segments of all departments including the equipment managers, the players, publicity people, advertising, promotion and marketing, and everything else relating to the team's day-to-day performance.

In-Game Marketing Coordinator

In-game marketing coordinators are responsible for ensuring that the venue's entertainment operates smoothly while fans are watching the game. The job of the in-game coordinator is similar to that of an event manager. They coordinate the logistics of events on the court, ice, or field that are part of the actual sport. These activities include dance squads, singers, and fan participants, such as fans chosen to shoot baskets for prizes during half time at a basketball game or the sausage race during the seventh inning stretch at Milwaukee's Miller Park.

In addition to supervising the performers at the arena, the coordinator also oversees the video board. They direct all of the content that appears on the video board during the game, and they consult with production to devise fun games for fans to participate in such as the "kiss cam" or the subway races at Yankee Stadium.

Despite the job title, much of what the job entails requires time spent in the office. Coordinating staff and event schedules, conferencing with event contacts, and managing equipment inventory are but a few of these tasks. Others include supervising supplemental staff at outside events, working closely with partners to coordinate fan development programs that focus on marketing the team within the community, and supervising the "street team." The street team is a group of young people whose job it is to promote the team at different events and activities within the local market. These part-time employees typically report to the in-game marketing coordinator.

In today's marketplace, sponsorship sales make up a large portion of the sports business industry. According to IEG Sponsorship Report, sports sponsorship spending by American companies rose by 3.9 percent to $17.2 billion in 2010. Sponsorship has shown consistent growth over the past 20 years. This type of increase has surpassed all other types of marketing like advertising and sales promotions. These traditional marketing methods in America are expected to grow only by three percent. Companies are recognizing the value of sponsorship, which in turn is creating many jobs in several sectors of the sports industry. The in-game marketing coordinator must be creative and have his or her finger on the pulse of what makes the fans happy. Because a large part of the job is creating and managing events individually, the position really requires a self-motivated individual who is comfortable working in a chaotic and challenging environment.

An in-game marketing coordinator can expect to make an average annual salary as follows: in the NHL, $27,000 to $43,000; in the NBA, $30,000 to $50,000; in the MLB, $25,000 to $45,000; and in the NFL, $34,000 to $55,000.

Marketing Director

Marketing directors develop the team's marketing strategy down to the smallest detail. Working in concert with marketing assistants and market research personnel, they approximate consumer demand and generate a brand image for the team. They also work to identify potential markets for saturation with advertising. In coordination with sales, promotions, and the sponsorship department, they scrutinize trends that indicate potential need for adjustment in services or brand image. Marketing directors also work with advertising and promotion personnel to promote the franchise's products and services and to attract more fans and consumers for team-branded merchandise.

Common responsibilities of the marketing director include: supervising sales and team marketing functions within the franchise's arena or stadium, working closely with the team's advertising agency, and generating new hospitality opportunities. In smaller-market circumstances (e.g., minor league teams or lower-tier sports), directors are sometimes tasked with responsibility for executive suites sales, maintaining marketing budgets, and working with outside departments on overall business strategy and execution of long-term business goals.

Most directors are tasked with maintaining and coordinating the implementation of budgeted goals and development of objectives for the team's marketing department. This includes developing strategies to maximize the value of the current inventory available for sale, including signage, print, Internet, radio, and television.

The director must be adept at developing both long and short-term strategies enabling the team to compete within the league in the areas of marketing, advertising, and (in smaller markets) ticket sales. To accomplish this, the individual must often research (or instruct staff to research) current and projected industry trends to ensure the team's marketing and sales strategies are in sync with the local market as well as the league as a whole.

Most marketing directors come either from lower marketing positions or public relations backgrounds. Most have at least a four-year degree, and many have a master's degree in fields such as marketing, business administration, communications, public relations, or advertising.

Salary levels often are calculated based on how much responsibility the marketing director has. A marketing director can expect to make yearly average earnings of $50,000 to $75,000 in the NHL, $65,000 to $95,000 in the NBA, $70,000 to $95,000 in the MLB, and $75,000 to $95,000 in the NFL.

Partnership/Sponsorship Account Manager

The business development account manager is responsible for maintaining solid business relationships with corporate sponsorship partners and the coordination of all contractual elements including radio and television, signage, publications, in-arena promotions, community programs, events, and hospitality. He or she is further responsible for creating proposals and sales tools to assist in the process of sponsorship renewal. Inventory often used by the manager to create individual sponsor partnership relationships includes merchandise, player appearances, media, stadium signage, special events (e.g., sponsorship summits), and direct/database marketing.

The account manager works day-to-day with clients to develop activation platforms and in-market promotions to help drive the sponsors' business and align with current property initiatives. Typically a team's key goals will include stimulating fan excitement and involvement and tapping into new demographic markets. Sponsorship managers work to provide the means for a corporation to deliver brand images to its target audience. It is therefore crucial that the account manager be fully cognizant of all sponsorship contractual elements and have a complete appreciation for the sponsorship partner's marketing and business objectives.

Individuals seeking a business development account manager position must have good communication skills and be adept at managing relationships. Account managers are the principle liaisons between the team and the sponsoring companies, and will therefore be either credited or blamed if their efforts result in a positive or negative experience for partner companies. Mediating disputes over contract elements and settling disputes over differences of opinion in a calm and rational manner is critical to success in this position.

The partnership/sponsorship account manager position garners the following salaries: in MLB this job at the entry-level could make as much as $40,000 to $70,000; in the NFL, $48,000 to $75,000; in the NBA, $40,000 to $68,000; and in the NHL, $35,000 to $62,000.

Partnership/Sponsorship Sales Executive

Candidates for sponsorship sales jobs typically have at least three to five years of sales experience either with a corporation, sports league, sports franchise, or a non-profit organization. These positions are full time and can be very demanding and stressful. Responsibilities of the sponsorship sales executive include identifying companies as potential sponsors and/or corporate hospitality customers through research and networking. The sales executive must also work to develop creative sponsorship proposals utilizing all available assets, including signage and printed materials such as programs, brochures, and tickets. In most cases, a team's largest sponsorship deal is the stadium naming rights deal.

The sales executive works closely with the director of sponsorships to ensure that all elements of the sponsorship agreements are accomplished to the satisfaction of the sponsor. Sales executives also work closely with the sponsorship account managers to administer available inventory to sponsors and forge relationships that are key to the sale renewal deals. Another key responsibility for the sale executives is generating sales leads by representing the company at local networking events.

Because this position produces additional revenue for the team, sales executives are usually paid more than account managers or marketing personnel. Often their compensation consists of a base salary

plus a commission based on a percentage of each sale. Teams generally seek self-starters with a strong work ethic, a winning attitude,
and the ability to be work as part of a team. In this particular position,
previous sales experience, particularly in sponsorships, is often preferred. This kind of job could make the following pay: MLB would pay
$55,000 to $100,000; NFL, $60,000 to $110,000; NBA, $50,000 to
$95,000; and the NHL's compensation averages $45,000 to $75,000.

Suite/Group Sales Account Executive

Sales jobs with professional sports teams are not limited to ticket
sales. Stadium suite/group ticket sales account executives generate and increase franchise revenue via sales of suites and club seats
to games by fostering relationships with clients through the use of
a current and prospective organization base. Acting as a business
entertainment consultant, the account executive maximizes relationship development while simultaneously coordinating the sale
of suite tickets, partial plans, group tickets, and promotional ticket
packages to local companies and individuals.

Reporting to the suite sales director, suite account executives follow up with clients or solicit appointments in order to make best
use of client relationship development while providing traditional,
theme, and special group ticket packages. Some additional responsibilities of this position include prospecting and generating leads
by cold calling potential clients, servicing clients and solving problems expeditiously for both existing ticket holders and prospects,
and meeting monthly and annual sales goals.

A suite sales position often requires a more creative approach
than that of general ticket staff, as increased ticket revenue often
results from the implementation of new programs and ideas. Most
suite sales staff members hold a bachelor's degree and often have
more sales experience in comparison to the general ticket sales staff.
As with any sales job, the suite sales account executive position
requires an independent, self-motivated individual who thrives in a
competitive environment.

MLB compensates a group sales executive in the range from
$39,000 to $75,000; the NFL, $48,000 to $80,000; the NBA,
$33,000 to $67,000; and the NHL, $30,000 to $63,000. This is a
position that relies on commissions for part of the pay. An individual who is adept at group sales can make the top range paid by
any of the leagues.

Team Marketing/Promotions Assistant

The marketing assistant is responsible for assisting in the development of all marketing initiatives and coordinating their execution. He or she also directs promotional programs, combining advertising with purchase incentives to increase sales for sponsoring companies. In an effort to establish closer contact with partners as well as consumers, promotional programs may include the use of direct mail, telemarketing, television and/or radio advertising, Web-based advertisements, in-store displays, product endorsements, as well as in-stadium signage. Purchasing incentives are normally part of these promotions and often include discounts, samples, gifts, rebates, coupons, and contests.

The marketing assistant aids the director in the execution of all marketing objectives, oversight of budgets, and compilation of advertising summaries for sponsorship partners. He or she may also supervise internship programs for the department if working for a larger market team. In addition, the assistant will typically function as the key marketing liaison with all vendors associated with product promotions at the stadium or facility. In some cases, this may also include coordinating with an outside advertising agency when such advertising is not done in-house.

Beyond the strategic and event management aspects of the position, there are game-day duties. These include oversight of sponsorship partners who may be operating promotional booths and/or events within the arena. The marketing assistant prioritizes maintaining a solid working relationship with the team's sponsorship partners, which, in turn, increases the chances for renewal when the time comes.

Marketing assistants typically hold a degree from a four-year university, and invariably have some familiarity with branding and brand management. As with other sports jobs, in which projects are always in flux and priorities are constantly shifting, being self-motivated and able to think on one's feet is critical to professional success. Hours may be long during the season, because assistants are expected to work not only during regular business hours, but also during the events themselves.

The following ranges of salaries for marketing assistants were gathered by surveying team personnel within the respective professional leagues. These salaries are not static and vary dependent upon many factors such as years of experience, education level, geographic region, and team reputation. A marketing assistant can expect to make $24,000 to $38,000 in the NHL, $30,000 to $48,000 in the NBA, $25,000 to $40,000 in the MLB, and $35,000 to $45,000 in the NFL.

Ticket Sales Account Executive

A ticket sales account executive is a great entry-level position for the person looking to get a foot in the door in the areas of marketing, branding, or sponsorship. Having a four-year degree and some sales experience or relevant internship are the best ways to get an initial interview.

This position requires a hard-working and enthusiastic individual who can properly communicate the team's overall value to its clients. Account executives must also be capable of working with fellow sales staff members as part a collaborative team environment. As a member of the sales and marketing team, sales executives are expected to follow up with all incoming leads in a timely manner and accurately qualify each contact, distribute relevant team-related information to potential clients, cold call prospects from targeted account lists, and generate potential leads. The primary goal of these tasks is meeting/exceeding an expected number of leads and, ultimately, closing deals. Account executives are expected to implement and sustain sales metrics to ensure delivery of clients over given time periods.

Ticket sales is a frenetic occupation that requires a great deal of time and energy, but those who are successful at it have an easier time moving up the organizational ladder. Thus it is a great opportunity to launch a career in professional sports.

There is a wide salary range in this particular job because much of the pay comes from commissions made. Candidates who are able to generate a lot of ticket sales stand to do very well in this job. In MLB, he or she could make $24,000 to $70,000; in the NFL, $28,000 to $78,000; in the NBA, $24,000 to 75,000; and in the NHL, $24,000 to $72,000.

Sports League Jobs

A job in professional sports, especially working for a professional sports league, is clearly something to which many people aspire. In both the United States and abroad, these sports jobs not only tend to offer better pay than those with individual teams, they also offer access to some of the most exciting sporting events. For many people there is nothing cooler than the idea of working for a world-class professional league.

If there is a downside to working for a sports league, it is that there is a limited number of professional leagues (and therefore positions) to be had. This makes the competition extremely intense. Professional sports league employees perform a wide range of different tasks, including marketing and branding of the team, sponsorship sales and the administration of those business relationships, updating and maintaining the league's Web site, event planning and management, and handling all of the logistics necessary to fostering league success.

Accounting Coordinator

Sports jobs are not much different from their counterparts in the "normal" corporate world. Like accounting and finance positions in the corporate setting, coordinators at the league level deal with cash flows, assets, liabilities, revenue, and profit and loss statements. What is distinctly different from standard accounting positions are the line items: things like sponsorship dollars, collective bargaining agreement (CBA) information and salary cap, raw salary data, depreciation and amortization of the stadium and/or the team's purchase price, television revenue, and league revenue sharing dollars coming from the teams.

The accounting coordinator is in charge of the daily cash accounting, which includes posting funds to the bank and reporting daily on the cash flow of revenue. The accounting coordinator will post daily ticket sales, generate invoices, and post daily cash receipts. He or she will also investigate or check in on unpaid ticket purchases. The accounting coordinator keeps ledger balances and reconciliations, and keeps track of monthly payment schedules for sponsor accounts and other revenue sources. If needed, the accounting coordinator will substitute for the accounts payable personnel. The accounting coordinator must be aware of the different laws that affect private profit making companies or nonprofit entities.

The accounting coordinator must have the minimum qualification of an associate's degree in accounting. He or she must be very proficient at Microsoft Excel and Word as well as other accounting software programs that are used in entertainment industries. Accounting coordinators must have excellent organizational skills, be extremely detail oriented, and posses sound problem-solving ability.

Accounting coordinators make more money at the league level and tend to have more experience than in other jobs. Relocation costs are often paid. Because people in finance have very technical skills the pay is based on experience and education. These positions are paid more than marketing and sponsorship. MLB pays from $68,000 to $90,000; the NFL, $80,000 to $103,000; the NBA, $60,000 to $84,000; and the NHL, $58,000 to $80,000.

Database Manager

Keeping track of sponsorship sales, media inquiries, marketing, advertising, public relations, team information, and fan activities and information are crucial for the success of a sports league. Without close scrutiny of these and other important areas, leagues (and teams) would risk missing vital information that might otherwise allow them to be more successful in their business ventures. The database operations manager for a professional sports league implements and maintains league database systems. This typically includes the oversight of customer relationship management (CRM) systems. Database managers must also secure, analyze, and report on all of the records and data sources that are maintained by the CRM system.

Database operations managers must have advanced computer skills, specifically those that relate to database applications such as PHP, Access, and SQL. These skills are critical because the position not only calls for analysis of the database information but also supervising the design, testing, and delivery of all system enhancements. The information extracted from the database is utilized to assist in the development of sales campaign strategies through a complete understanding of all available data fields and sources. This information ultimately allows for enhanced tracking of the efficacy of sales campaigns through quantitative and qualitative analyses. Database operations managers must also keep abreast of new data collection methods through all available outlets to help maximize efficiency and the accuracy in how data is both stored and collected.

Database operations managers working in sports must hold an undergraduate college degree and typically must bring at least three years of database management and/or sales experience. Although this is not a direct sales position, leagues typically offer annual incentive bonuses based on performance and measured results. Database managers pay ranges are as follows: MLB pays from $68,000 to $85,000; the NFL, $75,000 to $100,000, the NBA, $70,000 to $95,000; and the NHL, $60,000 to $80,000.

Legal Counsel

Legal counsel is another term for trained and experienced lawyers. In sports organizations, they are responsible for making sure contracts are fair to the parties involved and that the organization is legally protected from liability. Legal counsel oversees all the contracts of the organization, including collective bargaining agreements, sponsorships, revenue sharing, and marketing deals. Legal counsel also handles many other legal issues that can arise in a sports organization. These can be related to the employees, executives, or the company as a whole. Counsel may deal with breach of contracts, work stoppage clauses, mediation clauses or morals clauses, terms of agreement in unilateral or bilateral outs, territory of granted rights, category of granted rights, such as trademarks, right of first refusal, structured payments, preferred pricing agreements, rights fees, and indemnification of the organization along with other liabilities.

Most attorneys that end up working at a sports organization usually are hired from outside firms that are doing legal work for the sports league. Attorneys who maintain good relationships with the sports league or organization will have an easier time making the leap to working within the organization. Relocation costs are usually covered. MLB pays $92,000 to $115,000; the NFL, $95,000 to $125,000; the NBA, $85,000 to $105,000; and the NHL, $72,000 to $100,000.

Marketing Coordinator

The league marketing coordinator is typically responsible for supporting the marketing manager in development of marketing strategy, and often takes charge of the execution of the resulting marketing initiatives. The marketing coordinator also assists in scrutinizing budgets and compiling advertising summaries for partner companies. Coordinators seek to establish closer contact with partners and with consumers through a number of marketing, advertising, or public relations strategies. Similar to the team marketing coordinator, league coordinators also supervise the internship program within the department. Because of this, the assistant becomes the primary marketing liaison to all vendors associated with league

Everyone Knows

Personal Seat Licenses

A recent development teams have concocted to increase revenue is the Personal Seat License. A Personal Seat License (or PSL) offers the holder the right to buy season tickets for a given seat in a stadium or other sporting venue. This holder has the option to sell his or her seat license if the time comes that they no longer wish to purchase season tickets. Since the seat licenses typically increase in value, they can be seen as an investment for the buyers. For the teams, the PSLs are free money, plus they generally result in an increase in vendor sales—since anyone paying for a PSL is not likely to let his or her seats remain empty very often.

promotions. Sometimes this includes coordinating with outside advertising agencies in the event that the work is not done in-house.

Some of the league coordinator's primary responsibilities include assisting with the development of the league's various advertising campaigns; coordinating the formation of print, electronic, and environmental advertising with coworkers in the creative department; supervising the advertising budgetary follow-up and tracking of media purchases; assisting with development of various promotional programs connected to league-wide initiatives and public events; and helping to ensure league sponsorships are respected and validated both in the sporting venues as well as in the media.

A major requirement most sports leagues look for when hiring for this position is a bachelor's degree in marketing or sports management and, usually, two to three years of related professional experience. Other skills sought by many leagues include fluency in a second or third language, the ability to multitask while simultaneously prioritizing established goals, a willingness to work long hours, superior communication skills, and highly-developed computer skills.

This job is entitled to receive relocation compensation, which is often not done for other positions. Salary levels are based on the length of experience, level of managerial responsibility, education, and professional level of the sport (minor league versus professional league).

MLB pays from $35,000 to $50,000; the NFL, $40,000 to $55,000; the NBA, $35,000 to 55,000; and the NHL, 35,000 to $50,000.

Marketing Manager

Marketing managers supervise the development of the league's marketing strategy in minute detail. Leading a team of marketing assistants and market research personnel, they collectively estimate demand and generate a brand image for the league in a manner similar to their counterparts at the team level. In addition, they identify potential markets for advertising and other media assaults. In conjunction with the promotions and sponsorship departments, they scrutinize trends that could indicate the need for modifications of services or brand image. Marketing managers also work with advertising and promotion managers to implement strategies that best promote the league's products and services and to attract additional fans and increase sales of branded merchandise.

The primary difference between the marketing director positions on the league as opposed to the team level is the amount of money that is available to him or her. Leagues make (and subsequently spend) substantially greater money in marketing, sponsorships, and all other departments.

Professional leagues typically seek those with professional experience in marketing and/or communications to lead the team that devises the best brand image for the league. Some of the core responsibilities of a league marketing manager include development and execution of groundbreaking marketing programs and events (e.g., membership recruiting and retention), publicizing league-sponsored programs and events to the consumer base and various trade media outlets, identification and development of fresh business development prospects to increase revenue and/or promotional opportunities, and working in tandem with external agencies and internal departments (including advertising, PR, and event management) to maximize league marketing opportunities.

The minimum requirements for an individual seeking this position include an overriding passion for the sport, a bachelor's degree (typically in marketing or communications), roughly eight years professional experience in either marketing or public relations, a proven track record in development and implementation of strategic marketing plans (often at the team level), and the demonstrated ability to administer events and brand image.

The marketing manager position has a wide range of pay depending on experience, education, and whether the job is for a minor or major league team. MLB pay ranges from $58,000 to $85,000; the NFL, $70,000 to $100,000; the NBA, $60,000 to $95,000; and the NHL, $47,000 to $68,000.

Public Relations Manager

The public relations manager is responsible for writing press releases, holding press conferences on behalf of the league or organization, monitoring the team league or organization's Web site, and ensuring that the all team events are appropriately covered in the media. The PR manager also acts as a liaison between all sources of media, including the league's own network as well as local and national media sources and broadcast outlets.

The PR manager handles all facets of community relations. This includes overseeing the league broadcast plans, working on disseminating information to broadcast networks, and volunteering the organization to host charitable events where the team or sports organization can receive positive media coverage. These media appearances could include guest appearances and endorsements by players or coaches, product promotions, and giveaways, all giving the media access to information about the team or players, and by working with team statisticians and prediction tools to spin stories to the media. PR managers also ensure that the team is following the league rules and procedures when dealing with player statistics, scoring, and player benchmarks. The PR manager responds to inquiries from the general public and the media. He or she also handles media access to the league or team's players, coaches, and executives.

The less glamorous side of the public relations manager job is dealing with scandals or negative media stories that arise from player behavior—or the behavior of anyone else working for the team, league, or organization. The PR manager along with team executives decides how to handle negative press that affects players and the organization as a whole. The PR manager then spins the story to be released to the media.

Many PR managers have a minimum of a four-year college degree in marketing, communications, journalism, or a related field. In addition, some years of experience working in public relations are helpful when applying for a job. Most leagues or sports organizations have sports internships where candidates who are interested in getting into a sports-related field can get some experience before graduating from college or they can obtain a paid postgraduate internship.

PR managers are usually paid higher because of the revenue that they handle and the fact that they handle exposure of the league. This all adds up to a greater level of responsibility. Relocation costs are usually covered. MLB pay ranges from $47,000 to $78,000; the NFL, $58,000 to $85,000; the NBA, $45,000 to $72,000; and the NHL, $42,000 to $72,000.

Sponsorship Sales Manager

Sponsorships are a main source of revenue for sports teams and leagues. A sponsorship is defined as the equal exchange of resources between parties. A professional team and a company will choose to do business together because their goals for business are well aligned. The sports team is looking for sponsors who will make a financial investment into its organization. The sponsor wants to advertise their brand to the public in a way that is meaningful for consumers and that heightens the public's awareness of the company's products. By using a major sports team as the showcase for their products, sponsor companies are able to increase their revenue because consumers who are fans of the major sports team will associate the product with their team and buy it.

Each sports league handles sponsorships in a different manner. The NFL controls all of the team logos only when they are displayed equally. The also manage all big championships in the league such as the Pro Bowl, the Super Bowl, and all league trademarks. The NFL chooses what sponsorships a team cannot override: If the league chooses to do business with a certain beer company, for example, a lone team cannot choose to do business with another beer brand. In contrast, the MLB and NBA allow individual teams to sell whatever they want as sponsorships, the league's position notwithstanding.

Sponsorship sales managers often start their careers as sponsorship sales executives or account managers. Sponsorship sales managers run the sales and account management of the league and oversee the staff. They work with the VP on devising strategies to target companies. Managers also work with the teams to try and identify sponsors that the team is allowed to sell to.

Sponsorship sales managers have the important job of creating relationships with sponsors who market their products using the team's logos, players, or other representations. The sponsorship sales manager must have a very clear understanding of the goals of the sponsoring company partnered with the team. The team's players that advertise the sponsoring partners' brands must have the kind of reputation that does not tarnish the sponsor's image in the media or with the general fan base. More importantly, the team's arena or grounds, their logo, and their players that are advertising the sponsor's product must be able to generate revenue for both the sponsor and the team. The sponsorship sales manager must be able to identify and pinpoint the objectives of the sponsor's business and be able to create revenue-producing ideas that enhance it. He or she must be in close contact with the senior executives of the sponsoring companies and be able to customize business plans that reflect their vision for their product's growth.

In addition to the primary responsibility of maintaining a good base of sponsors, the sponsorship sales manager has to fulfill many duties that relate to sponsorship relationships. The sponsorship sales manager is responsible for making sure that the corporate packages designed for sponsors are being implemented. He or she has to make sure that the tickets as well as all signs in the arena and on the grounds are properly printed with sponsor names and logos. He or she must also check that they are placed according to the contract agreement. He or she makes sure that all facets of media—electronic, print, and Web site production—are done in accordance with the sponsor contract. Finally, the sponsorship sales manager supports the sales staff in fulfilling their sales goals while monitoring the budgets in place from sponsor revenue.

When the sports team or organization decides to approach prospective clients, the sponsorship sales manager has to prepare proposals to attract business from new sponsors. Sponsorship sales managers must be able to come up with innovative ideas to attract new clients, which will in turn generate money for both the sports organization and the sponsor.

The sponsorship sales manager must be an effective communicator both in print and verbally. He or she will often send memos and letters to clients and in-house staff that must be clear and concise in nature. These duties call for the ability to use MS Word, PowerPoint, and Excel. This managerial position also requires the candidate to be able to work well with people inside and outside of the team organization.

In general, a sponsorship sales manager must have at least five years of corporate sales experience in media businesses or in sports organizations. He or she must also have had some kind of sponsorship sales experience, or have worked specifically with coordinating sponsorship efforts for a business entity.

The sponsorship sales manager will make more money at the league level as opposed to the team level. Relocation costs are paid for this position. MLB pays from $60,000 to $75,000; the NFL, $65,000 to $90,000; the NBA, $65,000 to $78,000; and the NHL, $52,000 to $65,000.

Sponsorship Services Account Manager

Sponsorship services account managers are in charge of sponsorship sales accounts. They liaison with sponsorship partners to ensure their goals are being met by the team organization. Sponsorship services account managers also have to see that the sponsor's contract is being upheld. This may include making sure the correct radio spots are in place, the sponsor's signage is placed as agreed, the team's publications are featuring the sponsor's ads, and that in-arena and retail promotions prominently feature the sponsor's brand. Sponsorship services account managers also oversee any community programs or events that the sponsor wishes to support.

The sponsorship services account manager is the main representative that the sponsor deals with. These managers must be highly effective at managing relationships with people. Much like the sponsorship sales manager, the services account manager works to increase the revenue of the organization by ensuring that sponsor clients are happy with the team or league. If sponsors are satisfied with the sports league or organization, they are more apt to renew sponsorships. The sponsorship services account manager must be able to understand who the major advertisers are in his or her geographic area. These managers may be involved in writing proposals that convince sponsors to re-sign new contracts with the sports organization as well as be responsible for writing new proposals for prospective clients.

Sponsorship services account managers must posses a great deal of customer service skills. They must also be able to keep good relationships with current sponsors, try to ensure that revenue is growing through the sponsor relationship, and make compelling sales presentations. They must be able to identify and analyze market data and customer trends in the geographic location, as well as create proposals that target the sponsor's marketing goals while incorporating market data analysis. Sponsorship services account managers need to be able to work closely with sales staff and hand off accurate information to them for follow-up.

The sponsorship services account manager must hold, at minimum, a bachelor's degree in a business-related field. Most sports
leagues or organizations prefer to have a candidate that has had
some experience in the industry or working in corporate sponsorships. Because this position requires the candidate to deal with
large amounts of money, the pay is much higher than other jobs.
Relocation costs are often paid for this position. MLB pays within
the range of $47,000 to $59,000; the NFL, $50,000 to $65,000; the
NBA, $44,000 to $65,000; and NHL, $42,000 to $55,000.

Web Site Administrator

Web site administrators are typically responsible for the development and implementation of creative initiatives for the content on
the league's Web site. He or she is further responsible for overseeing the information on the site—primarily the conceptualization,
creation, and management of Web site content, as well as the writing of dynamic feature articles and stories. Accomplishing this often
requires attending some team practices or events, press conferences,
and other league activities. Sports Web site managers work closely
with myriad departments, league and team officials, players, and
colleagues to create and maintain the best possible Web site for promotion of the league.

On the Cutting
Edge

Web Affiliations

Web sites play an important role in a sports league's
marketing initiatives and in important the league's message with the teams that comprise it. In the early days of the
Internet, individual franchises operated their own sites, but over time
the team sites have been increasingly unified in their appearance and
content. Through this convergence, sports leagues are better able to
present themselves as a united front rather than a collection of loosely
affiliated (and occasionally maverick) individual franchises. In the process of monitoring the league site, content managers maintain league
message boards and blogs from a quality assurance perspective.

As with other Web-related positions outside of the sports indus-try, league Web site administrators update the league Web site either remotely or from the office. People in these positions coordinate the development, placement, and prioritization of the site's graphical user interface (GUI), features, revenue opportunities, and feature roadmap, or work with an outside agency to make sure that graphics meet the league's specifications.

The primary qualification that candidates must have to land a job as a content manager for a sports league is at least seven years of Web site content development and management experience. Leagues often look for other qualifications including the ability to work in a stressful, deadline-intensive environment; outstanding layout and writing experience creating copy/content on the Internet; a bach-elor's degree in computer science or Web-related field; and at least some meaningful experience in public relations, media relations, communication, and journalism.

Both at the league level and team level, Web site administra-tors are paid according to the amount of Web-related content they produce and their ability to work with software. MLB pay range is $55,000 to $100,000; the NFL, $63,000 to $100,000; the NBA, $55,000 to $95,000; and the NHL, $45,000 to $80,000.

Sports Facilities Jobs

Like other jobs in the sports field, facilities jobs are a growing seg-ment of the workforce. It takes many well-trained employees to fully operate stadiums and other sporting venues. Being affiliated with a major sports team carries a certain amount of interest or prestige for employees. These jobs tend to have a lot of competition as many people are vying for these highly desirable positions. It also gives an employee access to a major sports team and the players on that team at times, which is a huge extra benefit for those who are big-time sports fans. Despite the intense competition, with proper education and relevant experience, it is possible to get one of these jobs in the ever-growing sports entertainment industry.

Box Office Manager

The box office manager has the very important responsibility of maintaining the contents of the facility vault. He or she must be able to account for all the cash, credit receipts, and tickets in the vault.

He or she must keep the right amount of funds at the ticket windows for cash sales. The box office manager oversees all the counting of money and tickets at the end of an event and manages the ticket sellers in terms of cash drawer receipts. He or she takes care of the daily deposits and returns blank ticket stock to the ticketing department. He or she must accurately report all sales to the finance department. The box office manager also monitors sales through Ticketmaster and makes sure that there are no fraudulent transactions occurring with customers' credit cards. Other additional duties include taking care of gift certificates that are redeemed, raffles, and other small events that generate cash. In case there is an emergency, the box office manager can also fill in for the ticketing manager.

Concessions Jobs

Working as part of a concessions crew is usually a part-time event operations job. Most concessions jobs are hourly, part-time positions. As such, the requirements for being hired are less restrictive than other jobs. Candidates must be at least 16 years old, though at some facilities the age requirement is 18. Because many events are held during the evenings and weekends, concessions crews must be able to work flexible hours. Having prior food service experience is also preferable.

Many employees at a facility or venue prefer to work on the set-up crew. This crew is responsible for setting up catering equipment, supplies, and décor for the box seats at stadiums or event center. Catering crews retrieve and store all the necessary equipment. They also handle phone calls from suite attendants who put in food orders, as well as handle phone complaints from customers. Other duties include entering orders in a computer database, handling purchases, writing up invoices, and processing payments. Other concessions jobs include working at a food court or booth. These jobs require employees to work at a rapid pace during events, handle customers politely and efficiently, handle food according to safety requirements, and the ability to run a cash register.

Concessions jobs are very consistent in pay across all four leagues. Most jobs have overtime especially when there is an event. Suite attendants often make a salary plus tips. MLB pays minimum wage to $15 per hour, the NFL pays minimum wage to $18 per hour, the NBA pays minimum wage to $15 per hour, and the NHL pays minimum wage to $15 per hour.

Director of Operations

The director of operations is considered an executive position. This person reports directly to the vice president of operations who runs a sports venue or similar type of entertainment facility. The director of operations is responsible for overseeing the daily fulfillment of job duties by the event staff. He or she also has the authority to recruit and train as well as to fire staff. The director of operations has to develop and put in place sporting event policies that match the goals of the company. These procedures must be in sync with the operating procedures and operations consistent with the company's desire to be profitable and entertaining for customers. The workers that run the game night operations and coordinate events are under the authority of the director of operations. Therefore, he or she must effectively communicate to his or her staff the policies, procedures, and operational guidelines that the company wants. The director of operations must also resolve problems by coordinating with all the departments to make sure game night entertainment runs smoothly.

The director of operations is the front person who deals with the landlord or the facility personnel where the professional sports teams play. He or she checks that there are no conflicts with team schedules and procedures that the venue requires to be in place. He or she monitors the landlord/tenant relationship to make sure that the sports franchise staff follow the guidelines of the facility and that the sports team is happy with the facility and its features and services. The director, along with the marketing and presentations teams, food and beverage services, and merchandise shops all look to find ways to entertain the fans. Musical presentations by special guests and celebrities, visits from military personnel on special holidays, lighting effects, team cheers, organ music, and announcements are an essential part of what the director and the staff work at to keep fans entertained at sporting events. The director of operations keeps and updates a master schedule of all events. He or she is responsible for overseeing that backstage procedures, post-game events, fantasy or summer camps, and other special events all run smoothly.

The minimum education requirement that a director of operations must have is a bachelor's degree in one of the three areas: communications, public relations, or sports management. If he or she does not have the educational background, experience in the fields of public relations, communications, or event management will suffice. Sports companies much prefer to have directors that have combined several years of experience and education. People who still wish to apply for a director of operations job but do not have the necessary experience or education must be able to prove that they have the right skills and talents to do the job.

A director of operations can expect to make the following salary ranges in the four leagues. MLB pays from $87,000 to $120,000; the NFL, $100,000 to $125,000; the NBA, $82,000 to $106,000; and the NHL, $71,000 to $92,000.

Engineering/Building Maintenance Jobs

The engineering crew is responsible for building maintenance and repairs. The crew will usually be able to perform work duties related to systems in the building such as plumbing, electrical, structural work, and patchwork. As with many jobs that require a large amount of manual labor, engineering and maintenance jobs frequently involve lifting, carrying, or moving/positioning objects exceeding 50 pounds. Maintenance crews are required to bend frequently in order to work in small spaces. Engineers and maintenance workers may also assist with related maintenance and upkeep of the stadium, the grounds, the offices, the parking lots, public areas, and any other projects; in addition, they help with the process of converting the arena for different events.

Engineers and maintenance crews are required to service requests and check on supplies and equipment. Engineers or other maintenance supervisors are responsible for inspecting jobs and for ensuring compliance with facility standards and building and safety codes. Supervisors may also have to regularly make inspections of buildings and grounds.

Engineer and maintenance crews will need to have a significant background in construction, facilities maintenance, or related fields. The position requires employees to have the ability to operate heavy machinery. Engineers are required to have a B.S. in engineering, construction, or a related field.

Engineers often make overtime depending on the project they are working on. MLB pays $25 to $32 per hour, the NFL pays $20 to $40 per hour, the NBA pays $16 to $30 per hour, and the NHL pays $14 to $24 per hour.

Facility Manager

There may be overlap between the facility manager and various director jobs. Larger venues have both a director and a facility manager and need both positions to run the sporting events efficiently. Sports facilities that host smaller sporting events usually have just the facility manager. The facility manager's primary responsibility is to create and manage an operating budget that turns a profit for the company. The facility manager works with financial and other team personnel to produce sports entertainment that is within the expense budget and will create profits. The facility manager oversees staff that sells time for events and shows at the facility. Trade shows, company meetings, or alternative sporting events are just some of the kinds of events that staff can book space for at the facility.

In addition to managing the financial welfare of the facility, the facility manager oversees the hiring of private contractors that maintain the arenas, fields, or grounds of the facility. Electrical contractors, building contractors, specialty builders, and groundskeepers are some of the contractors the facility manager hires. He or she may even be responsible for buying specialty products like dirt, clay, or turf for fields and hiring consultants for ice production at ice rinks (if the facility has the capacity).

Facility managers must have at the minimum a bachelor's degree in marketing, communications, or a sports business related field. Facility managers that have experience beyond five or six years in managing events are considered desirable candidates. Facility managers often are promoted or hired into the position after having had experience in marketing, sports sales, group ticket sales, or sponsorship sales.

Some facilities are large enough to have both a facilities manager and a director of operations. Those venues pay less to the facilities manager since the position has fewer responsibilities. Salaries can vary widely depending on the job responsibilities and size of the venue. MLB pays from $64,000 to $120,000; the NFL, $68,000 to $125,000; the NBA, $56,000 to $105,000; and the NHL, $50,000 to $92,000.

Guest Relations/Event Staff Jobs

Guest relations staff are responsible for ushering VIP clients, club patrons and suite owners to their seats, and checking tickets. Candidates must be able to deliver a high level of customer service and be able to handle difficult clients. Guest relations staff are always attuned to the latest updates occurring at an event, because they are provided with an electronic device that allows them to receive information before it is announced.

Guest relations attendants sometimes provide tours of the facilities for guests. As such, they must set a positive tone for the tour since they are representing the facility. They may also handle reservations for the tours. Guest relations attendants should have the tour script memorized, and be able to interact with guests on the tour with skill and poise. A thorough knowledge of the sports teams and the venue is typically required for employees running the tour.

Facilities, venues, and stadiums do not typically require staff positions to have undergraduate degrees. Companies do like their employees to be articulate, personable, and able to interact with the public. Creating a positive experience for fans is the primary role of guest relations attendants and tour guides.

Guest relations and event staff jobs pay from minimum wage to an average of $22 per hour. Some staff is salaried. Many staff can make overtime when there are events. MLB pays minimum wage to $22 per hour, the NFL pays minimum wage to $35 per hour, the NBA pays minimum wage to $20 per hour, and the NHL pays minimum wage to $15 per hour.

Night Manager

The night manager oversees the overnight custodial staff and manages the facility overnight. He or she hires, trains, and takes disciplinary action against night staff. The night manager's primary responsibility is maintenance and prep work for the next day's events. This may include responsibilities like planning for upcoming events, budget and expense control, and coordinating events on the master schedule. The night manager is wholly responsible for building maintenance and repairs.

The night manager must be able to speak both English and Spanish and otherwise communicate effectively with the staff. Being that the night manager is a union contracted position, he or she is expected to have experience working in an environment where he or she understands and enforces union rules. Building maintenance and repair are of utmost importance to the safety and comfort of guests and fans. The night manager is responsible for making sure that these duties are clear to his staff and implemented with efficiency. He or she must be able to read and interpret safety manuals and procedure manuals for his staff to follow. Furthermore, the night manager may be called upon to create and design manuals for the staff.

(continues on page 68)

INTERVIEW

People Want to Give Back

Dave Perricone
Assistant Professor, Sports Management, Centenary College, Hackettstown, NJ

How did you come to enter the field of professional sports?
I went to Robert Morris University in Pittsburgh, Pennsylvania, and
majored in sports management. In my senior year I had an internship
with the New Jersey Devils. During my final semester the National
Hockey League (NHL) All-Star game was in Pittsburgh. I volunteered
for a hospitality company, picking up players and even getting to help
transport the Stanley Cup! I got to know the president of the Devils,
talked with him, and let him know I was interested in a position with
the organization. He told me to call when I graduated. I did, and took
a job as a staff assistant, which was a foot in the door.

I worked in this position for two years, answering phones, assisting the operations, public relations, tickets, and other departments. I
moved into the merchandising department as the assistant merchandising manager, and eventually as the senior director of merchandising. Here I was director of the merchandise catalog, overseeing its layout and design as well as preparing financial reports, supervising staff,
and selecting and reordering merchandise. In the time I was there we
won three Stanley Cups, so I am proud to say that I have three championship rings. Some athletes go their whole career without winning
one. Also at that time the New York Yankees, New Jersey Nets, and
Devils were all owned by the same organization, so I oversaw a joint
Nets-Devils catalog.

In 2006 I knew I wanted to further my career. I was always interested in teaching, and there was an opportunity at a local college to
teach adjunct at night. I did this while maintaining my role with the
Devils by day. In January 2011, I was hired at Centenary to oversee
their sport management concentration. Some of responsibilities include teaching, advising the students, and securing internships.

**What traits are essential to success in the field of professional
sports?**
You have to get involved. Grades are important, but you have to volunteer and build your résumé. While attending Robert Morris University, I worked four years with the Pittsburgh Pirates baseball club. This
gave me an opportunity to see firsthand what it was like working in
professional sports. I also worked for our college athletic department.

This also gave me a chance to see how an athletic department functions. During my junior year we worked with the Cleveland Cavs in promoting a Western PA Day. This project taught me how important it is to have a sales class and how to interact with customers. These opportunities helped me prepare for my future in sports. By getting involved as much as possible you can see what you like and don't like. Also, getting involved gave me a chance to network and meet some successful people in our industry.

Network as early as possible. Be different. I tell my students to print business cards that say "Sports Management Student." Also, separate being a fan from being an employee. Remember this is not a nine-to-five job. There are no holidays—teams play on Thanksgiving and Christmas—and you might have to work a 10-game home stand without a day off. Take business courses. Know accounting. Take a sales course and a public speaking course, as you'll have to market yourself and will be called on to make a lot of presentations.

Should the sports industry professional be tapped into any technological or social trends?
Use Facebook and LinkedIn to network. Keep track of social media such as Twitter. Read journals such as *Sports Business Journal* and *Athletic Management*, which have articles to keep updated on technological developments. For instance, many teams are using a new electronic card for season tickets. Stay one step ahead of the industry by networking with other teams. Talk to students, teachers, and peers to keep informed of trends.

What is the importance of mentoring in the professional sports industry?
It is very important. In my freshman class I assign each student one person in the industry to connect with on LinkedIn. One student had a fellow who worked for a marketing company who helped him find a job after graduation. I have a teacher from 1988 who is still my mentor and with who I am still in contact. At the Devils office, senior employees often took others under their wing. The industry is like a fraternity. People want to give back. They want to help others get into the industry, because many of them have been helped at some point in their careers.

What are some challenges particular to the sports industry professional?
Every major league team has a recognized name. It's like a fishbowl: everyone is looking at what you do. In the merchandising field, I

(continues on next page)

INTERVIEW

People Want to Give Back
(continued)

learned to keep my personal preferences out. Even if I didn't like an item, I had to order it if I knew it was going to sell. It can be tough to move up in this industry. There are so few professional sports teams that if you want a PR position, for example, there are very few spots available. You may have to decide if you are willing to relocate. Sports pay isn't high, and there is a lot of demand for jobs. You may have to start with a low salary, working long hours and balancing family concerns.

What do you enjoy most about your work in the professional sports industry?
The greatest joy in merchandising is going to games knowing that fans bought from us—seeing the fans with equipment, or the little kid's expression when he gets something. In teaching, it is seeing students succeed. One graduate told me, "I wish you were here four years ago, because you taught me how to network." Watching students learn, have professional success, and staying in contact with them are the greatest joys.

(continued from page 65)

A night manager position typically requires at least a high school diploma, though managers are encouraged to obtain an undergraduate degree. Night managers must also have experience in the field. The night manager must be an effective communicator and supervisor who is able to handle a myriad of problems with managing employees. The night manager must also be able to liaison and work with other departments in the facility. Finally, he or she must be able to appreciate the late shifts that come with the job.

Night managers can make the following salaries in each of the four leagues: MLB can pay from $40,000 to $65,000; the NFL, $45,000 to $68,000; the NBA, $42,000 to $65,000; and the NHL, $35,000 to $60,000.

Security Jobs

Security officers are responsible for maintaining a safe environment for guests and fans by providing a secure facility. This includes being on the lookout for theft or vandalism. They also help fans or guests who have had items stolen or lost. Security guards also check for fire risks and try to avoid this happening. They also check for individuals who enter the grounds or facility illegally. In addition to controlling access to the venue, officers also act as greeters while directing crowds and maintaining crowd control. They provide security for lockers used by employees to store their personal effects, issue new uniforms, and oversee uniform changes for lower level operation employees. Security officers may also do daily inventory management or cycle counts. When unresolved complaints arise, security officers will refer the complaint to their immediate supervisor.

There are some minimum qualifications one must have in order to be considered for a security officer position. The candidate must be at least 18 years old; be verbally proficient in English and able to speak and write intelligibly; have a cell phone or a landline phone where supervisors can reach him or her easily; be able to work flexible hours, including days, evenings, weekends, or holidays; and possess the ability to act calmly and quickly in the event of an emergency. In addition, they must pass any state training before employment. Many venues will assist otherwise qualified employees with this requirement. Candidates must have a clean criminal record and will be subjected to background checks before employment. If all above criteria are successfully met, security officers will receive an official license upon hiring.

Security officers are able to make overtime especially when events are going on. Some security officers draw a salary instead of an hourly wage. Security detail can expect to make the following in the four leagues: MLB pays $15 to $25 per hour; the NFL, $20 to $30 per hour, the NBA, $15 to $25 per hour; and NHL, $12.50 to $25 per hour.

Sports Event Coordinator/Event Manager

An event coordinator/manager works directly with two other managers at a venue: the director of event operations and the director of operations. The primary responsibility of the sports event coordinator/event manager is to manage all non-team related events at the stadium and/or event center. Many venues or stadiums have exhibition centers or other attractions within the venues. Event coordinators or managers oversee the booking of these events like trade shows, all-star games and corporate meetings. Event coordinators/managers make sure that all booked events run smoothly.

The events coordinator/manager works closely with the director in several key areas for the facility. He or she is involved in the advertising strategies of the facility. The events coordinator will often be responsible for working with outside advertising firms. He or she may have to summarize advertising reports for the managing partners, and will work with vendors who do promotions at the facility. He or she may also oversee the intern program for his or her department if the organization is large enough to support extra staff. Event coordinators pay close attention to consumer reports and marketplace data on consumer tastes. In conjunction with the director, the event coordinator will strategize on how to create entertainment for the fans based on research data that they have analyzed.

An event coordinator/manager is required to have a B.A. or B.S. in sports management or a related field. He or she must also have had at least two years of experience managing events or in facility operations. Because an events coordinator works closely with many people inside and out of the organization, he or she must possess good organization skills and be able to multi-task. As the events coordinator/manager deals with many vendors and clients, he or she must be articulate and must have good writing skills. Being able to use Microsoft Office is necessary for success in this position. Finally, event coordinators must be able to work flexible hours according to the events planned at the facility. Coordinators may have to work days, evenings, weekends, and holidays as needed.

Sporting events coordinator managers usually are paid partly by commission. This means that pay may vary widely. MLB pays $34,000 to $65,000; the NFL, $43,000 to $79,000; the NBA, $31,000 to $69,000; and the NHL, $28,000 to $65,000.

Vice President of Operations and Services

The operations vice president reports to the president of facilities such as sports venues and exhibition centers. The operations VP is responsible for overseeing all operations and business conducted at arenas and sports centers. He or she is responsible for employing people who have strong leadership abilities and are creative in their thinking. These employees run the business in a manner that maximizes profits for the sports arena or center. Employees are charged with providing sterling customer service and offering entertainment that enhances the experience of the guest.

The vice president of operations and services cannot be hired without a bachelor's degree. It is often preferable that the VP has a graduate degree in an operations- or business-related field of study. Often the VP will be expected to have 10 or more years of experience in managing a sports arena or center. In order to be successful, the operations VP must be able to show that he or she has demonstrable organizational skills. He or she must have an aptitude for verbal and written communication. The VP of operations will be able to manage his or her employees by being able to have good interpersonal skills. Lastly, the operations VP must be good at public speaking because they will have to give presentations regularly.

Operations VP jobs exist both in the corporate and sports side of the business. These job skills can be acquired through the corporate side and then applied to a sports-related position. Employees who are in lower level jobs can move into an operations VP position. However, employees who possess the skills necessary to be an operations VP but are in another field of work can cross over into the sports-related job.

Vice president positions can expect to earn within the following salary ranges according to each league: MLB pays $94,000 to $124,000; the NFL, $105,000 to $145,000; the NBA, $92,000 to $120,000; and the NHL, $82,000 to $100,000.

Chapter 4

Tips for Success

It is important to realize that accomplishment in any of the individual jobs within this industry depends primarily upon a congenial and collaborative personality. Like the athletes themselves, if you want to succeed in the professional sports game, you have to know how to interact with others to work toward a common goal.

Professional sports organizations apply a "teamwork" approach to their operations, so employees must work in concert to maximize the experience of their patrons. Of course this often requires an employee to swallow any negative feelings toward his fellow employees and bosses, as well as show tolerance towards disrespectful clientele. You must always remember that sports are a leisure-time activity that depends entirely on customer satisfaction.

Finding a Job in the Professional Sports Industry

As with any industry, the best and most expedient method for finding a job in professional sports is through connections. And though the old saying "It's not *what* you know, it's *who* you know" is not altogether true (having relevant skills, experience, and education certainly helps), having a connection can help you to get your foot in the door and prove to be as invaluable as a stellar résumé or a degree from a top university.

Unfortunately, those without friends or family in high places must resort to "pounding the pavement" in order to find an employment opportunity. While the old-school methods of job searching (e.g., job boards and classified advertisements) are still one way to go, they have largely given way to more modern methods. There are many online sites that post openings for jobs in the professional sports industry. In addition to those sports industry-specific sites, you might also consider more traditional career-assistance sites, such as Monster.com, Careerbuilder.com, and Craigslist.

Training and Education

Getting some type of training and education is the longest route, but it is the surest way to get into this industry. It is very difficult to get ahead in the sports industry or even get a foot in the door without some kind of training or education in the field.

Many sports organizations are looking for a unique skill set when they are recruiting new employees. Some of these key skills are: your ability to understand sports advertising and branding, being creative at promotions that bring in revenue for sports organizations, being knowledgeable about sales techniques that work, having a knack for identifying potential new markets, and having the ability to find revenue streams that make sense for the organization. Having some idea of how to market products and services via the Internet is also useful.

Other necessary skills include having some knowledge about how the front office runs, and knowing who the employees are and their various job descriptions. Being able to use the industry lingo will be helpful when communicating with colleagues. Understanding how community relations enhance the sports business and benefit the organization and customers is a key skill to have as well. Finally, being able to deliver value-added customer service will help boost your chances of landing a sports organization job.

Professional sports teams and leagues want to hire candidates who are already trained. They are looking for prospective hires that have marketing skills and can produce revenue by selling tickets, by managing event planning, and by acquiring sponsorships. You cannot get a well-paying job in today's sports industry without having some kind of training. Look for training programs that offer courses in sports management or sports marketing to boost your skills and enhance your knowledge base. You need to be thoroughly trained and ready to be indispensable to an organization if you hope to get a job in this industry. As you train, you will also meet people in the business and have the opportunity to network with professionals in the field. Maintain a list of all the contacts you make and stay in touch with them often.

These programs often give a varied training program that will offer courses that teach the necessary skills for jobs in such areas as player personnel, venue and stadium management, media and community relations, group and ticket sales, game operations, sponsorship, sports marketing, and merchandising. Many training programs will help you get hired at almost all of the major sports businesses out there. Some of these include: the NFL, MLB, NHL, NBA, NASCAR, and the NCAA. Minor league organizations are also great places to find work. Many people interested in working in the sports industry decide to get a bachelor's or master's degree to better their chances at getting the sports job they want.

In the field of sports management and marketing, professionals plan and use business tactics that help the sports teams and organizations run smoothly. This includes the operations of the business, the handling of the athletes, and the dealings with customers. Students who enroll in sports management degree programs can expect to find work as sports agents, managers, and administrators. If you choose to go the route of getting a professional degree in sports management, you will be knowledgeable in several areas of the sports field. For example, depending on what you plan to focus on, you can expect to take courses that teach you the essential information to work in marketing, promotions, and finance, as well as in a supervisory capacity within an organization. Participants in these programs will either earn an associate's or bachelor's degree in sports management.

Writing Your Sports Career Résumé

The job market in the sports industry is very competitive. Many people are vying for the very same positions that interest you. One way to get a head start is to have a good résumé. You will need to construct a sports career résumé that is relevant to the needs of the prospective sports organization you want to work for. Your résumé needs to catch the employer's eye and hold his or her interest. Keep in mind that sports industry employers receive a great number of résumés for any one position they may have available. You need to make your résumé stand apart from the rest.

Accurate Contact Information

Your résumé should list your contact information at the top of the page. It lets the interviewer immediately identify who you are and how to contact you quickly. Your ultimate goal is to be the candidate getting a callback. You need to make sure that is easy for the interviewer. List your mailing address, cell phone, and landline numbers, and all of your e-mail addresses as well. Do not include information on your Facebook or Twitter accounts. Your information should only pertain to your professional profile.

Keep It to the Point

Because employers have to read through many of these résumés, make sure that your information is brief and to the point. Do not embellish or lie about your skills. This can be detrimental to you getting the job if your credibility is hurt. Organize your résumé in a way that is easy to read and to follow skills, dates, and the places where you gained skills. A résumé with precise information indicates to the prospective employer that you care about how you make an impression on others and that you want to do a good job.

A concise résumé will have information organized in a way that piques the employers' interest. A good way to ensure this can happen is to record five or six skills, talents, or achievements. These advancements need not be directly connected to the sports industry. Sports industry professionals place high value on past experiences such as sales via cold calling, restaurant service and bartending, and other such jobs that demonstrate a candidates's ability to interact with the public and handle pressure-filled situations. By placing these directly under your contact information, you are guaranteeing that the interviewer will spot what you can do immediately. It is also better if you help the person reading your résumé to process the information you wrote down. One way to do this is to group information according to the subject it is addressing. For example, all education and training information should be together, all job information should be together, and so forth. Having these subsections can also make it easy to reference information during the interview or at a later time. It is not unusual for sports career résumés to be longer than a page. However, try not to exceed two pages. You need to carefully delete any information that is not relevant to the job you are applying for. If you need to keep data, try combining your subject matter to conserve on page space.

Keep Your Résumé Current

If your job skill sets change, be sure to change them on your résumé immediately. If you recently graduated, make sure that you update your résumé to indicate the type of degree or certificate you received. It is better to organize your data chronologically. Take the time to re-edit each section of the résumé accordingly. Recreating the résumé may be necessary if you had a job change, finished school, or completed an internship. Highlight relevant accomplishments. Again, if the résumé is longer than two pages, either combine some information or delete it completely.

Exaggeration Not Recommended

Do not dress up your résumé with false information. Most employers are going to check your dates, experience, and references to see whether they are accurate. These people are in the business of hiring people who can do the job. Period. If a prospective employer finds you untrustworthy based on your résumé, you probably will not be hired. Double check your start and end dates of jobs. Check over graduation dates and look over the skills you listed.

A polished and professional résumé will not have any spelling errors, grammatical errors, or typos. There are several ways to guard against these. One is to have someone else read over your résumé and check for errors. Another is to read the document backwards, starting from the last word on the bottom of the page to the top.

When you make note of your skills and experiences, be specific in what you can do. For example, if you managed sponsorships, you can write down the exact amount of sponsorships you sold. Similarly, if you have increased your ticket sales over the year, make a note of the increase in percentages or by amount if space allows.

Uniquely You

Many sports careers require the candidate to have a winning personality. Jobs especially in sales and customer service need people with charm and patience to deal with the public. When possible, communicate your ability to be personable and charming without sounding unprofessional. You want to sound sincere and friendly, not pretentious or bombastic. By communicating your love for sports and your dedication to the sports industry, you may be able to impress the employer. This can work especially for people who have little or no job experience in the sports field. You need to show that what you lack in experience you can make up for in enthusiasm. Remember, however, that professional sports is a big business like any other, and that the real key will be how you balance this enthusiasm with an ability to stay grounded, to maintain focus, and to dialogue openly with athletes, coaches, and owners.

Be Accessible

As you maneuver the minefield of job-hunting, you will find that you may end up with several versions of your résumé. This is a necessity in the sports career industry. Because of job competition you want to always stay current, relevant, and available. Keeping your résumé contact information current—updating your skills, training, and experiences—and even switching up your references could all be helpful in the long run. Some sports industry professionals even suggested having several versions of your résumé to best fit with different positions. One could highlight sales experience, for example, if applying for a job in public relations; another could highlight volunteer experience if applying with the community relations department.

Acing the Interview

One good way to ace your interview is to use several of the tips provided in this section. Public speaking skills are very useful when it comes to interviewing. Also, if you are interviewing for a competitive position, having speaking skills that set you apart from other candidates is a definite plus.

You are able interview because your résumé was a good sell to the employer. He or she already knows that you have the necessary skills; they know what your experience is, and where you were educated or trained. Impressive as your education, background, or credentials may be, if you cannot impress a prospective employer with a professional attitude and amiable personality, your chances for getting a job offer are negligible. The following suggestions will help you to maximize your chances of finding employment in the professional sports industry. Some of these tips may strike you as obvious, while others may be new to you. Regardless, heeding these basic rules will help put you in the right frame of mind to ace your interview.

Before the Interview

A simple but unique tip that may work is to think of your interview as if it were a date. Laugh at the interviewer's jokes, exchange stories if they want to do so, and agree with them if they gripe about something. Be friendly, congenial, and polite. Smile and be enthusiastic. Do not talk about bad job experiences or other employers in the business.

Also, try practicing your speaking skills by counting numbers instead of speaking before going to the interview. Listen to your voice modulation and focus on your eye contact and your stance. Using numbers instead of words to practice allows you to gauge your body language. Use a mirror to practice or ask a colleague to practice with you.

Always end your answers to questions with a period, not a question mark. Ending your sentences with a question mark makes you appear unsure of yourself, wimpy instead of confident. Try practicing by counting numbers again and listen to how you end your sentences, then try answering some questions with words and see if the questioning tone creeps back into your voice: "I want this job because I have the skills?" Try saying it with a period. Try practicing saying these sentences with periods over and over until you get it. Sounding positive and confident in an interview is always helps and never hurts.

On the day of your interview, plan to arrive five to 15 minutes ahead of time. Map out the route to the interview and make sure you time it to arrive with extra time. Dress to impress. The way you dress should be consistent with the position you seek. At the minimum, you should wear a business suit or equivalent attire. When in doubt, always err on the side of overdressing. It goes without saying that you should be well groomed and coifed, and your attire should be neat and pressed.

During the Interview

As you are greeted, look confident. You should stand up, hold a firm gaze, smile, and give a firm handshake. An interview could take place in a conference room, someone's office, or even the company cafeteria. Do not let this throw you off. Wherever the interview ends up being, wait until you are offered a seat. Usually the interview will be held in an office. You may want to take a look around the interviewer's office to gather clues about them. Perhaps there is a book or calendar that you have read or used. Or maybe his or her diploma is from the same school that you graduated from. Looking for things you have in common can help make the interview easier. Shared interests can serve as great conversation openers, particularly in the field of professional sports. Casually mentioning how you became interested in athletics or relating an anecdote of a memorable game can help relax the atmosphere. Do not touch or pick up any items in the office.

Interviewers will often offer you water or a beverage. It is best to politely decline this.

Once you and the interviewer have dispensed with the chitchat, immediately let he or she know that you are very interested in the job. Tell him or her that you are very confident in your abilities to do the job. Using words like *I can* or *I will* is a good way to convey how confident you are about your abilities. This lets the interviewer know that you are a good bet for this position. Also, it works well with the person if they will be your immediate boss. It lets him or her know that you will make their job easier.

During the interview there are some general tips that can help it go smoothly: Be polite. Always remember that you are being watched. From the very moment you arrive, the interview has begun (whether or not the interviewer is actually present). Being prepared about the company's jobs and people that work there is a plus. If you show up knowing the names of the people with whom and for whom you will be working, as well as the nature of their particular jobs, you will seem both studious and diligent. Preparation demonstrates enthusiasm and is likely to impress the interviewer. Before you walk in the door you should have familiarized yourself with the position, the job requirements, and the expectations for the role. If you have done this, then every time you answer a question you should be able to provide examples as to why you are a good fit for the position.

Do not get cocky. If you tell the hiring manager that you are the best thing since sliced bread, you will be toast. Check your ego at the door. Be humble, but not self-deprecating. The only thing worse than an egomaniac is someone who is complacent, so act like you want to be there.

Relax. Remember to take a moment to breathe and collect your thoughts before answering questions. Do not be in a hurry. And if you do not quite understand a particular question, ask for clarification before answering. Follow the interviewer's lead: if your potential supervisor is very businesslike, you should also keep your demeanor entirely professional. On the other hand, if he or she is more conversational, your responses can be a bit more relaxed.

Do not mention money. If the interviewer does not mention it, you should not either. And while it is a good idea to be prepared to answer a question about salary requirements, try to delay a compensation discussion until you have been made an offer.

Pause for effect. When you speak, use pauses before you answer the interviewer's questions. This is a technique that people do not use, but it is effective. It also says a lot about your confidence level. It also makes the listener anticipate your answer as one that will be relevant and interesting.

Do not exaggerate or embellish your experiences. Hopefully nothing on your résumé is padded, so they will not have an opportunity to grill you about something that is not true. Honesty, especially in an interview, is the best policy.

Be ready to answer any question. The employer will want to ask you questions like these: "Where do you see the company in five years?"; "Describe a goal you have set for yourself recently"; "Can you describe the workplace environment?"; "How would you describe your managerial style?"; "What is one weakness you have?"; and "How do you manage difficult people at work?" In the sports industry, questions may even address your philosophies of team building, communication between athletes and managers, and the role of the media in professional sports. Industry leaders want to see candidates with holistic understandings of professional sports: not just its business components, but its overall place in the cultural landscape. These are not easy questions, so come prepared with answers before the interview. If the interviewer asks you something that you do not know how to answer, do not fumble along searching for a response. Say you do not know. Again, honesty will be the better route. The reason the employer wants answers to questions like these is because he or she wants to make sure you are really interested in the organization. He or she has heard you say it already, but now these questions help him or her gauge your true interest.

It is perfectly acceptable, and even encouraged, that you also ask questions in the interview. At the end of most interviews, you will typically be given a chance to do this. You should be able to come up with at least one intelligent question, or you run the risk of seeming disinterested. Ask probing questions that will allow you to zero in on what the organization *really* needs. You will know you have struck a chord when a hiring manager starts harping on a subject (or a project that has gone untouched for months). Sports industry professionals often like to talk about their organizations and may even go on for a while. It is okay to just sit and listen as he or she waxes nostalgic. Here are some good questions you can ask your prospective employer or the interviewer: "What is your organization's most current business challenge for the company or department?"; "Can you tell me about how you delegate tasks?"; "What type of employee works well with you?"; "I'm glad to hear that teamwork is highly valued in your company. How does your organization company evaluate team performance?"

Remember to answer the questions the interviewer is asking instead of giving answers you want to feed him or her. Most interviewers are busy and probably have a packed schedule, or may have limited time to spend with you because they need to meet with other people in the company. Give them your information concisely. Provide relevant details of experiences or training that you have had. Sports industry professionals value internships; if you have one on your résumé, be sure to elucidate what it managed to teach you. Show that you understand the business of sports is filling seats; industry leaders want to know that you can view sports as a part of the entertainment industry, and know that ticket sales are of foremost importance. But do not give them every small detail. Attention spans are short these days, so be aware of how much you are saying. Look for clues from your interviewer that you need to end your answer and move on. He or she may nod a lot, look at their watch, or check their cell phone, and he or she may also look away from you.

Focus on what the interviewer is relating to you so you can tailor your answers to what he or she is saying. Listen for the use of industry or company buzzwords. Also think about what positions seem important to the employer and what skills and talents are needed for those positions. Use visual cues yourself to let the interviewer know that you are interested: smile, nod, raise your eyebrows, or try sitting forward. Also use phrases like, "Interesting, can you tell me more about...?"

Just as you are looking for cues as to whether your answers are too lengthy, you should also be looking to see how the interviewer is reacting to the content of your answers. Keep track of whether he or she seems puzzled, is taking notes on what you are saying, is holding eye contact, is nodding, or whether he or she is leaning away from you with arms crossed.

Expect to meet with more than one interviewer. Employers often like to see how the people you will potentially be working with receive you. You will probably meet with both supervisors and subordinates. Remember that the interview is still going on. You are still being watched, so do not let your guard down. Do not hold up the interview by getting into personal conversations with someone you know. This may give the impression that you think you already have the job. Always have extra copies of your résumé to hand out to anyone who asks for one. As you move along the line of interviewing, try to keep track of the next interviewer in the process and the ones you have met thus far. Remember to keep your cool. Stay confident and polite. Many sports businesses will run you through several interviews to see how well you hold up under pressure. The whole business of round robin interviews is also to see how employees will deal with you during (sometimes very long) workweeks. By getting this far in the interview process, it must mean that you have impressed the important people. The interviewers and hiring manager want to see how well you fit with their organization. You may need to repeat your information several times. This can get tiring. Hang in there. Everyone is just trying to get to know you. That means that something about you has impressed the right people.

After the Interview

There have been instances when a candidate aces the interview but fouls up the after-interview. The following tips will guide you towards handling the after-interview etiquette.

Before you leave the interview, ask for contact information from each of your interviewers. Usually larger organizations will have business cards or their information will be on the company's Web site. After a couple of days, compose a short e-mail to each interviewer thanking them for the opportunity to interview with them personally and their firm. By following up quickly you will demonstrate your enthusiasm and anticipation for a job interview.

If a company really wants you on the payroll, a manager will probably make you an offer. Do not obsess over something you should have done or said during your interviews. The company will most likely overlook minor flubs on your part if they really feel you can handle the job. Oftentimes, immediately after your interview, the company is not sure you are the right person for the position. They may still need to interview other candidates and talk it over amongst themselves. Therefore, your post-interview responses are very important to keeping you in the forefront of the minds of your interviewers.

Send a thank you note or e-mail. Using an old-fashioned note card is a nice way of leaving a lasting impression on your interviewers. A handwritten note with a personal recollection of something you spoke about to the interviewer can make a strong impact. Do not use cutesy note cards with animals, flowers, or people. Use a simple, elegant card that seems professional. Do not go on into detail about the interview or try to analyze how you did in the interview. Never apologize for something you could have said or done better in the interview. Hiring managers always appreciate a thank-you note. It is a crucial element that you should not forget.

An e-mail is better than sending nothing. Some organizations may prefer Internet communications with candidates. You can always check before you leave if it is appropriate to send a personal note or an e-mail.

Now comes the hard part: waiting for a response. People are often worried about getting a job in a tight job market. The sports industry is a competitive one, and it may take you several attempts to land the job you want. You may have aced the interview, but companies change their minds about needing personnel all the time. Do not continue to contact the manager for a response. Displaying patience is very important at this stage. Hang in there you will hear soon enough.

Advancing Your Career

Getting a first job in sports is a difficult feat. There are many people applying for the same job you are interested in because you all want the same thing—a fun, challenging place to work around sports teams and athletes. Do not give up hope. With persistence and tenacity you will find the job for you. If your job search is becoming frustrating, here are some ideas to get things going in a positive direction. Sometimes changing direction or taking a new tack towards a sports career job can get you to your desired position in the long run.

Internships

One of the first things you can do to get your career started is to look for an internship in a sports career field in which you are interested. Sports teams and organizations offer many internship positions, usually to college students, who fill many internship opportunities every year. Most internships last for a summer or a regular school semester. Some interns will be given a lot of latitude, while others will be closely supervised. Depending on the employer, interns can be given a surprising amount of responsibility or very little. It varies. Try looking for an internship that fits the career interests you have. Send the word out that you are looking for an internship. You may be surprised to find out who has a contact with a sports job. Try tapping your coaches, teachers, and school personnel. Research the biographies of some of your favorite coaches, analysts, or agents to learn how they developed their careers. Perhaps their paths can inspire your own and provide ideas for internships. If you see an internship that is not exactly aligned with your interests, take it regardless. The end goal is to form new relationships with players and personnel, and any means that helps with this is good. Getting any internship is better than not having any experience at all. Perhaps working several internships will give you a combination of skills you need in the sports field.

If cold calling about an internship, try to speak to the internship coordinator if the organization has one. Always ask what duties you are expected to perform as an intern. This will alert you to whether the internship is a good match for you. Let the coordinator (or another contact) know what kind of skills you have or where you worked so he or she can come up with a good fit for you. The pay offered by sports organizations for internships varies greatly. Some may offer a small stipend while others expect interns to work for free. Your focus is on getting your "foot in the door," so do not worry about pay right now. You may have to forgo a lower-level pay job for a good unpaid internship, but you will reap the career benefits in the end. Look for internships that are a good fit to your professional sports interests. You will have a better job skills match for your résumé and more success getting into your niche in the sports field. The ultimate goal is that the sports organization winds up hiring you after your internship runs its course. If you excel at the tasks the organization gives you during your internship, you will have a valuable reference in the sports industry that you can put on your résumé.

Starting an internship is similar to starting a new job. Be sure to find out exactly what is expected from your employer. This is the opportunity for you to make a good impression and hopefully get hired. Always try to exceed expectations with the projects or tasks you are assigned. Listen to the advice from the people with whom you are working. Do not try to make too many new suggestions. You are a rookie in the business so you are there to learn. Once you have done some projects and learned how to operate in your environment, perhaps you can start making suggestions. If you complete your projects or tasks before the deadlines, you can approach your manager to give you new assignments to work on, or perhaps you can request to shadow someone in a department that interests you. You will probably have an opportunity to circulate in several departments or at least meet the heads of those departments. Keep business cards or get contact information from everyone. An internship is just the kind of opportunity you need for further job connections and networking.

Occupations in the professional sports industry are divided here into seven general areas: partnership/sponsorship, ticket/suite sales, public relations, marketing/promotions, legal, technology, and facilities.

Partnership/Sponsorship

The partnership/sponsorship department deals with selling the sport to the public in creative ways. These include sponsoring events and partnering with companies to produce branded or licensed products. Sometimes this department is involved in product design. Sponsorship officers are responsible for inventing campaigns to promote its teams and brand-name products from relevant markets. Partnership/sponsorship professionals have to be able to sell their ideas on television or in print. Often they will also take an idea to retail stores. This department may have an overseas unit that deals with sales in foreign countries. Sponsorship coordinators in this department may work on booking commercials, infomercials, and celebrity endorsements. Sponsorship officers may work on customer service, sales, and even design packaging. Officers may be responsible for acquiring airtime from networks, cable, or foreign TV companies. Coordinators or officers may also specialize in acquiring print and media advertising space. This department is charged with bringing in large revenues by putting out specialty concepts that draw customers to the athletes and the product they are endorsing. Sponsorship account coordinators must be able to execute contracts efficiently and smoothly after the deal has been reached.

Sponsorship managers will also need to work with all the other departments to coordinate promotions. Partnership/sponsorship has to work with broadcasting, marketing, community relations, and ticket sales. Professionals in this department must also create promotions, programs, and community outreach programs that will raise the level of entertainment for the fans and also help partners' businesses succeed. This department has to report back to the executives of the company on the sales records and to forecast what the sales revenues will be for the seasons to come.

Success in the department of partnerships and sponsorships is predicated on your ability to make and sustain personal connections. Seek to cultivate long-term professional relationships; many people fail when they try to secure a high number of one-time sponsorships rather than focusing on a limited number of long-term ones. You must build up a sense of trust with these sponsors so that both they and you—and the organization you represent—can take a proactive approach in discussing exactly what you want out of the agreement. Cultivate a conversational atmosphere where everyone can speak on equal footing, and reinforce the notion that sponsor and organization are positioned for joint success.

Be sure to research the organizations with which you are dealing. This goes hand-in-hand with the need for open, honest communication. Familiarize yourself with their financial record. Investigate the soundness of their business ethics. If they are a sporting goods company, have they employed child labor? Such things may be of concern to your organization. Finally, be sure you have an "exit strategy" in case a sponsorship does not work out. This is usually done in the form of a contractual clause that allows for a swift division of both parties. If you maintain a clear and open dialogue, however, such a severance should be entirely avoidable.

Ticket/Suite Sales

Agents or representatives who work in ticket or suite sales are responsible for the direct sales of tickets or box seats for the sports organization. Agents in this department may sell tickets as group packages, season ticket packages, partial ticket packages, luxury suites, or other kinds of ticket packages. Agents will also have to come up with clever promotions to promote ticket sales or to maintain current sales and generate repeat sales. Representatives in this department need to be very proactive in generating ticket sales and must always be on the lookout for ways to get new or increased ticket sales. Agents or representatives must be able to manage multiple customer service relationships simultaneously. Sometimes, representatives will have to be present at games to assist with special promotional events. Agents will need to attend weekly sales meetings and training and development sessions, and may also have to attend other departments' meetings. This entire department has to provide excellent customer service at all times. Agents will often be asked to meet or exceed weekly, monthly, and long-term sales quotas for season ticket sales, group ticket sales, and partial ticket package sales. Finally, account coordinators need to be well versed in record-keeping and the computer programs that are used to manage ticket sales. Sometimes the department agents are expected to work in the evenings during sporting events.

As with many jobs in the professional sports industry, the competition for any sales position—particularly one that specializes in such high-end items as season ticket packages and suite sales—is intense. The best way to prepare yourself is to take an entry-level sales position, even if it is in another field entirely. Prospective employers want to see salespeople who have worked to create their own opportunities, just as they will work to create sales opportunities for the organization. During this time you should track and document your sales achievements, develop a personal philosophy of successful sales, and understand your strengths while working to correct your weaknesses.

Bear in mind that selling luxury items such as suites and season tickets is very different than selling most other things. You will be dealing with customers who expect attention to detail with every facet of the transaction. It takes more than just an aggressive sales approach or a history of past success to work well in this sector of the sports industry. Potential employers will want to see that you are articulate and personable, capable of giving premium service from initial contact to final sale.

Public Relations

Public relations is one of the departments that is growing in the sports industry. This is because there are so many media avenues available to the public. Sports public relations professionals act as liaisons to integrate and coordinate information to the press from the team. PR professionals also spin stories from the team to the media. This can be in the form of player profile information, statistics about the player(s), or data about the team. Public relations specialists also are integral in increasing the team's exposure to the public. If the athletes are visible to the public, then the fans will want to come to the stadiums.

Public relations specialists usually have to work very long hours, sometimes seven days a week during the sports season. Large sports organizations will have several people in the PR department. Smaller sports venues may only have one or two people. PR specialists are responsible for everything that goes to print, including game schedules and programs, as well as overseeing print stories, and meeting with news outlets. PR specialists who work for college teams or minor league organizations may also write copy for the press, prepare press briefings and deliver them, and handle team records.

One of the very important jobs that PR specialists handle is providing information on tragedies or scandals. Public relations professionals all agree on one thing: it is always best to tell the truth. If you are faced with a crisis with an athlete or coach, trying to "spin" the story to mislead the public will only help you lose fans. Telling the truth preserves your credibility, which is the most important currency in this field.

The practice of public relations utilizes an incredibly diversified skill set; as such, it is one of the easier fields to break into from a variety of backgrounds. Written and oral communication skills are absolutely key. No matter what your current job, if you want to get into public relations you will have to demonstrate sound writing abilities. Employers will want to know that you are a nuanced, tactful person, capable of creating narrative arcs about your client team. The journalists you rely on to generate buzz recognize a good story when they see one, and it will need to have a beginning, middle, and an end. Have you drafted a new quarterback? What is his background? Has he had to overcome any adverse situations to reach this point in his career? Public relations professionals must intuit key details and amplify them for their audience. They must be able to see opportunities for nontraditional relationships, such as promoting a star athlete in a fashion magazine to reach an entirely new demographic. This storytelling ability, an instinct to see individuals and teams in a larger context, is what separates average public relations professionals from truly successful ones.

Best Practice

Big Fans

Give the fans of your team their 15 minutes of fame. Ask fans to send in photos of them wearing fan gear or when they attended a game or promotional event. Post these photos daily on the company Web site with clever captions. This will draw customers to your Web site where you can offer them incentives to buy more tickets or suites.

Marketing/Promotions

Marketing department consultants are required to look over all sponsorship proposals and brand marketing plans that the sponsorship department plans to execute. Consultants in this department also need to recommend sports marketing programs that will boost ticket and suite sales. Marketing consultants also manage brand marketing so that the company maximizes profit from its name and image.

Marketing *executives* work with external clients to oversee that the messages going out to the public are aligned with the company's key values and are being disseminated to the appropriate consumer target market. Marketing *analysts* will look for the best media placement for the sports organization and try to arrange contracts with a particular brand or product that accomplishes this. Marketing *managers* are charged with developing multi-year goals and objectives, also known as a marketing plan, that will increase brand awareness and therefore reach sales goals. Marketing departments are held accountable for these plans and are expected to yield measurable results. Marketing *associates* may be responsible for continuing open communications with external clients (such as ad companies or casting agents) so that the department is aware of decisions being made that may affect the face of the organization.

Marketing managers are charged with overseeing all the marketing and promotions for a certain region or area. Managers must also take a leadership role in creating new sales or revenue opportunities for other departments. For example, the marketing manager needs to work with the sponsorship/partnership department and other departments to deliver a seamless presentation of the face of the sports organization to all markets. The marketing manager also oversees how the advertising department uses materials to ensure consistency in the organization's name brand.

Making advances in sports marketing requires understanding the nature of your fan base. Promotions that may have worked 10 or 15 years ago may not be as successful with a new generation of fans. Marketing professionals agree that it is key to isolate a target market—in this case, a particular segment of your fan base—and cater to them. The media landscape has fragmented everything to a series of niche markets, and the marketing managers of the future must be savvy enough to align themselves with customers rather than products; they will engineer experiences for their customers, not just push merchandise onto them. In the field of professional sports this might mean allowing for greater customer (fan) interaction with the players via social media sites such as Twitter or partnering with "social game" providers to make games for mobile devices based around a player or team. In short, marketing managers who wish to be successful in the coming years will have to make fans feel less like spectators and more like participants in the drama of their favorite team.

Legal

Most jobs in the legal department require a law license. There are several types of jobs that lawyers can do in a sports organization.

A contracts specialist drafts and negotiates basic sports contracts with coaches, professional athletes, and sports federations. This lawyer also helps marketing managers and counsels partners by reviewing marketing, sponsorship, and branding contracts. This type of attorney acts as a consultant for clients by supporting them in understanding contract rights. Contracts specialists will have to prepare reports that update the company as to what contracts are signed and what is to be signed. These attorneys also handle administrative duties such as processing of contracts, filing and assisting with mailing, and preparing return letters.

Senior counsel coordinates the negotiating, drafting, and filing of media-related contracts, distribution agreements, content acquisition agreements, and technology agreements. Senior counsel also handles legal research such as FCC and FTC regulations, privacy policies, online property, and network related issues. Senior counsel may serve as a legal advisor to the human resources department in employee-relations issues. Should lawsuits arise over labor disputes, senior counsel oversees these cases on behalf of the company and works directly with the human resources department.

Counsel may also have to assist athletes or other employees by giving them legal advice as needed. Or counsel may have to advise the company on how to handle employee-related problems. Senior counsel is also responsible for handling litigation, arbitrations, and mediations that involve the company. Counsel also handles case discovery, negotiations, and case resolutions. Counsel is needed to conduct workshops that advise on the best practices of employee relationships and legal compliance should lawsuits arise. Counsel's main job is to minimize the company's legal exposure, and they must keep up with developments in case discovery and case law.

Unlike other sectors of the professional sports industry such as sales, the roadmap to success in the legal area is not quite so clear-cut.

Besides the requisite educational requirements, potential candidates need to have passed the bar exam in their respective states. Though sports agents are not required to have a law degree, most do. Know that even when dealing with athletes through a legalistic framework, you must still be equipped to handle egos and oversized personalities. Much like entertainment law, sports law requires innate people skills and the ability to leverage power. You will be expected to fight on behalf of your client against some of the toughest negotiators out there, a challenge not for the faint-hearted.

Technologies

The system administrator or the IT generalist provides computer support (phone, data, and Internet hardware and software support) to internal and external clients. He or she is set with the task of making sure that the computer operations are maintained and running at all times, as well as seeing that day-to-day computer use and support for sporting events is running smoothly. IT generalists will retrieve, analyze, and resolve computer problems for the organization. They will usually run diagnostics to find problems and work as quickly as possible to resolve them. The systems administrator may also have to be present to assist with the coordination of vendor activity and sports events.

On the Cutting Edge

There's an App for That

Many companies are creating applications (apps) that highlight their services and products for smart phone customers. Talk to your IT department about creating an "app" specifically for your customers in your department that highlights ticket packages, game times, and upcoming promotions.

Success as an IT generalist in the world of sports depends upon your ability to study and analyze data. Perhaps more than other businesses, sports organizations meticulously track the data of their employees—that is, their players. Fans want this information readily available on Web sites and apps for portable devices. Marketing teams depend on it to generate promotional content. Be open to working with other areas of the organization. Do not ensconce yourself with your IT peers. Spearhead collaborations with the public relations department to design social media sites or team-based apps for portable devices. Marshal your knowledge of computer systems to improve upon existing databases—any means of making data more easily accessible will be looked upon favorably by your employer, your peers, and the fans of your team. Remember that fans expect Web sites to be continuously updated and visually stimulating, so be proactive in suggesting improvements to its design or ways to make it more user friendly. In all, IT specialists in the sports industry must look beyond their day-to-day duties of maintaining the modern computerized workplace, seeking instead to integrate their skills with the team as a whole.

Facilities

This department is sometimes referred to as the athletic field operations unit. It coordinates the daily operation of stadium, field, or floor usage. Facilities also oversees any camps that may be going on throughout the year for high school and college athletes.

The facilities worker assists in day-to-day preparation and breakdown of equipment for home athletic events. He or she also provides any support needed on game day. Facility workers may supervise interns and student day workers during camps, contracted events, and the main athletic events. Facilities workers also coordinate and monitor facility maintenance under the supervision of the assistant director. Facilities workers also may be responsible for food service for employees as well as the concessions during games. Facilities workers sometimes collect, inventory, and send out equipment for repair and maintenance.

The assistant director oversees all housekeeping and maintenance on the sports facility campus; manages the department budget, oversees the execution of vendor contracts, and works with the IT department to make sure technology support is in place for internal and external clients; works with all the other departments to ensure proper maintenance and upkeep of a clean sports stadium, as well as the office complex; and manages the maintenance of the security systems. He or she may also oversee the security staff on campus if there is not a separate safety department; coordinate the maintenance of the athletic grass/turf fields, ice rinks, or wooden floors; and schedule the jobs of the interns and oversee their term at the sports facility. The assistant director and the facilities manager both coordinate vendor contracts and manage the department's budget.

The facilities manager develops, implements, and disseminates the building safety policy, the maintenance policy, and the policies regarding use of equipment and vehicles on the sports complex premises. He or she manages external agreements for rental equipment needed for event promotions at the stadium. The facilities manager also coordinates event operations with the marketing and sponsorship departments should any promotions happen on game days at the complex. With the assistant director, he or she manages the parking attendants, ushers, and concession stand workers. The facilities manager also conducts a weekly walk-through of the sports complex to make sure all of the above systems are in working order. He or she holds meetings regularly to keep staff updated on upcoming events, changes in schedules, or any other business that needs attending to.

No matter from what field you are coming, rising through the ranks of the facilities operations department will depend on your ability to work hard and be proactive in making changes to improve efficiency. Trust your instincts. If you see an easier way to do something, suggest it. Sporting events run on an extremely tight schedule, and input is encouraged. Show that you can work independently and that you are capable of prioritizing tasks. If you can prioritize your own workday, employers will trust you to prioritize the workdays of others. Monitor the condition of equipment and stay ahead of repairs. Contentiousness is highly prized in this sector of the sports industry, as there is such a vast amount of equipment that one or two operations managers cannot keep track of it all. Showing you are cognizant of the needs of the department is the quickest way to rise to a facilities leadership role.

Keeping in Touch

The Personal Touch

Sending a personalized card with a handwritten note is a wonderful way to let a customer know that you value her business. A thank-you note for buying a suite or a package of tickets creates a positive impression for your client. A handwritten note is a personal touch that shows that you are thinking about your client. If you do not have nice handwriting, have cards made with your personal notes and sign them. Everyone appreciates getting a letter or card in the mail.

Getting Ahead in the Professional Sports World

In any industry, the key to moving through the ranks is by using a combination of performance and attitude. The key to securing a promotion lies in a superlative work ethic and an organized, direct approach. Start by visualizing where you would like to be in your career and the path you will need to take to accomplish your goal. Decide where you would like to be in the next six months, the next year, the next five years, and so on—and figure out what it will take for you to get there. Then you need to write down these goals. List all your goals from the easiest to the most challenging. You will add new steps as you build on your sports career action plan.

Most often, people who are drawn to sports careers have a love of the game and want to spend their careers working within that sport. Much like an athlete who speaks about having specific goals he or she wants to achieve though a combination of motivation, tenacity, and integrity, you will need to have a rigid plan to negotiate the highly competitive sports field.

Get the Word Out

Let your superiors know your career goals. They are often aware of opportunities before anyone else. By gaining their support in your career goals, they can help you achieve them.

Use all of your networking resources, both Internet and otherwise, to build your contact list. Plan on attending professional development opportunities such as sports conferences, workshops, and conventions that are focused in your area of interest. There are many sports leagues or trade associations that conduct meetings on a consistent basis. It is a definite plus if you are staying current with the latest changes in your sports niche. Also use the people you know (e.g., teachers, coaches, professors, and advisors) to build contacts. If just out of college, use your campus career center for leads. Let your friends and family know that you are looking for work and the type of work you are looking for. You never know when someone will hear something and pass it on to you.

Be Smart

One of the surest methods for impressing one's superiors is displaying exceptional diligence and mastery of your current position. Take an active leadership role that lets you shine and shows your superiors that you can deal with extra responsibility. You will not only gain valuable experience by learning new things, but you will also have the opportunity to get your hard work noticed. By staying in touch with those in your work environment, you can gain valuable access to information about upcoming promotions, trends in professional sports leagues and growth within the organization. Encourage your superiors to give you extra projects or tasks that will help you work towards your goal. Ask them what it takes to achieve the promotion you are looking for and then work at acquiring those skills.

Getting a promotion is about working hard and making sure the right people notice. By planning, networking, and communicating, you can facilitate this process. By letting your manager know that you are interested in positions higher than yours, you are giving him or her the heads-up that you are looking to get promoted. If you let them know what your current accomplishments are, you have already begun laying the groundwork for the inevitable. Asking your current manager what suggestions he or she has to help you get started on the path to a promotion will give you a leg up on the competition.

Most sports organizations will give you a yearly performance rating. This is an excellent opportunity to ask for a professional development plan that outlines how you can reach your promotional goal. Multitasking is now a buzzword that affects all of us in the workplace. For better or worse, we all have to learn how to multitask to some degree. Thankfully the age of technology helps us somewhat. If you can learn how to manage multiple projects, clients, and tasks, you will be able to do more than others and thus get ahead far quicker than others. The harder you work, the greater your chances of being rewarded with a merit increase or promotion to the next level. Eventually, doing more than expected will likely result in a promotion—whether within your current organization or by finding a better opportunity.

Be Tenacious

Your outlook will affect your approach to getting a promotion as well. You need to show tenacity in your job tasks. You have to be proactive and positive. This means that you make time to meet with your clients (if you are involved with sponsorship and promotions) more often, or you have lunch dates with coworkers or you spend time training the new interns, which in turn gives your boss a break.

Stay Positive

Staying positive does not mean you have to be a Pollyanna. Sometimes having a sense of humor about situations can help lighten the mood. Sports is a form of entertainment, and remembering this (while never losing sight of the business end) will help give you this necessary levity. This also helps if there is a deadline for your department to meet and everyone is working late. You can be the guy or gal that brings in the coffee and donuts for the late night session! Take the advice from your colleagues on how to do better next time if you happen to make a mistake on the job.

Play Nice

Having integrity on the job is always a plus. Be fair and honest with your clients and coworkers. Do not assume people are out to get you. If your colleagues need help getting out of a tough situation, offer a hand. Your boss will notice your willingness to pitch in and help. This is also a good quality for a leader to have.

Trying to succeed in a very competitive atmosphere can seem like a daunting task. Keep trying. When one path fails, try another. Perhaps getting a job in a similar field as a springboard to your dream job will help. Work hard, stay the course, and use the tips provided above. You will get that dream job in the world of professional sports.

Chapter 5

Talk Like a Pro

The sports industry, like all industries, has its own vocabulary. Some of these terms are related to the fiscal and business side of professional sports, others cover the rules and regulations of different games, and still others touch on the logistical demands of promoting and hosting sporting events. Study them all so that you too can "talk like a pro" when you make the interview circuit or join the industry.

above the line (ATL) marketing   Traditional advertising through large media outlets.

activation   The additional costs to a sponsor, beyond the basic costs of the sponsorship rights, for promoting the sponsorship to its fullest potential. These may include additional advertising, inclusion of the sponsorship in existing advertising, or other marketing campaigns.

aisle seats   Seats located at the end of a row, directly next to the aisle.

All-Star Game   An exhibition game featuring a sport's top players, often selected by the fans.

ambush marketing   A promotional strategy whereby a non-sponsor attempts to capitalize on the popularity or prestige of a property by giving the false impression that it is a sponsor. Usually employed by the competitors of a property's official sponsors.

aspirational media   Media planning/market research term typically applied to media which reflect the lifestyle ambitions of a particular consumer group.

assets   The places owned by an organization that have the potential to display a corporate brand name or logo. These places may be a part of a building or venue, in official publications or literature, or may be placements in media. These assets have a value that can be determined, priced, and sold to sponsors.

Astroturf   Artificial grass used on many professional sports fields.

attendance   The number of people present at a particular event.

audience   Individual, group, or market segment to which a sponsorship is directed or focused.

badge   Like a ticket, a badge can be used to enter an event. Typically the badge can be attached to a lanyard where it can be easily shown to event staff.

banners   Signage produced as temporary advertising.

bar code   A bar code is an optical machine-readable representation of data, usually found on the back of a ticket or on a product label.

barter   The exchange of goods and services without the use of cash. In the media market, this usually refers to the acquisition of media time or space in exchange for merchandise.

BBB   An acronym that stands for Better Business Bureau. Disgruntled consumers often complain to the BBB.

below the line (BTL) marketing   Non-traditional advertising outside of major media platforms. A common example is direct mailing.

between the pipes   A hockey term referring to playing goalie.

biscuit   Nickname for the hockey puck.

blink or blinkers   A counterfeit ticket.

box office   A place where tickets are sold for an event.

brand development index (BDI)   A measure of how well a brand sells in a certain market.

brand equity   A measure of the influence a brand has in swaying a consumer's decision to purchase a product based solely on the brand.

brand extension   Putting an old brand on a new and different product.

branding   A sign of identification or personality. A brand is the heart of what a company or organization represents and embodies all the positive traits the company wants to portray.

broadcast Electronic transmission of information by radio, television, or Internet technology.

broker An individual who can legally resell tickets to an event.

bundling Refers to the grouping of various assets into packages which are then sold to the sponsor as a group. As an example, a bundle might include the opportunity for a sponsor to display a banner at the finish line, a logo on participants' t-shirts, passes to a VIP box, and perhaps a picture with the team or an individual athlete.

buried Another name for bad seats.

burners Tickets used to enter the event but once inside the ticketholders sit somewhere else. Burners are usually used by people with access to a sky box.

business-to-business (B2B) Sponsorship programs aimed at corporate purchase/awareness as opposed to individual consumers. May also refer to contacts between co-sponsors and even sponsors of competing teams, creating business between the parties.

busted order When a customer's ticket order goes unfilled.

capital sponsorship Sponsorship developed from the ground up, including development and implementation of capital initiatives and projects.

category exclusivity The right of a sponsor to be the only company within its product or service category associated with the sponsored property.

cause marketing Promotional strategy intended to link a company's sales campaign directly to a nonprofit charitable organization. This typically includes an offer by the sponsor to make a donation to the cause after purchase of a product or service. Money spent on cause marketing is a business expense, not philanthropy, and is expected to show a return on investment.

Fast Facts

Matching Points

The United States Tennis Association fostered a particularly successful cross-promotion of American Express and Polo Ralph Lauren Corporation at the 2010 U.S. Open. Consumers who spent $100 on their Amex cards at the tournament were rewarded with a $50 gift card for use at Ralph Lauren stores.

championship event   A sporting event wherein a championship is determined. The Super Bowl is the most famous example, but every sport has a championship game or series.

co-sponsors   Sponsors of the same property.

commissioner   The chief executive of a sports league.

conference   Groups of teams within various leagues, often formed around common geographical locations.

consignment   The process of using a third party to sell something you own. For example, a season ticket holder may use a ticket broker to sell seats to a game or performance they are unable to attend themselves.

convention and visitors bureau (CVB)   A resource sports event planners use to bring events to their community. The bureau provides services including, but not limited to, hotel and restaurant information, calendar of events, visitor guides, housing, and attraction and shopping information.

corporate campaign   A corporate marketing campaign which addresses general company objectives and targets a large audience, rather than focusing on the sale of a specific product or awareness requirements. Sponsorship is the most successful vehicle for such campaigns.

cream seats   A term for great seats.

cross-promotion   A joint marketing effort conducted by two or more co-sponsors using the sponsored property as the central theme (e.g., beverage manufacturer and retailer, credit card, and commercial bank).

demographics   The breakdown of a population into statistical categories.

direct response   Promotional media activity that enables consumers to respond directly to the advertiser via post, telephone, e-mail, or some other method of communication. Often successfully used in conjunction with sponsorships.

double header   A baseball term referring to two games played on the same day.

draft   The annual system by which teams of various leagues select players who are ready to enter the professional level.

dugout   A baseball term referring to the seating area for team members when they are not on the playing field.

duplicate tickets   A counterfeit ticket made to look like a real ticket.

e-marketing   The use of online devices, such as Web magazines, bulletins, and newsletters

e-tickets   Electronic tickets. Usually purchased online and sent to the buyer via e-mail.

economic development   May occur at the state, regional, or municipal level, or in public-private partnerships organizations that may be partially funded by tax dollars. These organizations explore new economic generating opportunities while working to retain their current business wealth.

economic impact   Net change to the economy caused by activity involving the acquisition, operation, development, and use of sport facilities and/or services.

endorsement   Payment to a performer—either an individual or team—to provide a testimonial, make personal appearances, function as spokesperson, and/or appear in advertising on behalf of a company.

end zone   A football term referring to the 10-yard-long area at both ends of the field. Touchdowns are scored when a player enters the zone while in control of the football. If a player is tackled in his own end zone while in possession of the football, the other team gets a safety.

evaluation   The process of assigning a value to each asset within a property's inventory. This value is usually based on the number of impressions (i.e., the number of times people see the logo) the property can deliver. Unique sales opportunities at an event, media coverage, and the likelihood of an event or property to appeal to a specific demographic, will all impact the evaluation of the inventory.

event   A gathering, festival, athletic event, performance, concert, or other function that provides a sponsor opportunities to display a corporate brand or logo. The event may be professional, such as a sporting event or concert, or it may be charitable, such as a fundraising run or showcase. Both types of events have the potential to attract sponsors.

event management   Process by which an event is planned, prepared, and produced. It encompasses the assessment, definition, acquisition, allocation, direction, control, and analysis of time, finances, people, products, services, and other resources to achieve stated objectives.

event manager   Individual responsible for oversight and coordination of every aspect of an event, including research, planning, organizing, implementing, and evaluating every facet of that event's design, activities, and production.

event marketing   Promotional strategy linking a company to an event.

event pre-sale tickets   Tickets available to fan club members or some other group, prior to their becoming available to the general public.

expansion team   A new team added to a sports league.

face value   The price printed on the ticket, but not necessarily the price you're actually charged for the ticket.

facility fee   A fee added to the face value price of a ticket.

facility guide   Document or online listing of sports facilities located within an area that can be utilized for hosting sporting events. These guides typically include details of facilities including seating capacity, floor dimensions, lighting available, air/heating system, etc.

fair territory   A baseball term referring to that part of the playing field bounded by the first base and third base lines, home plate, and the playing field fence.

fan club ticket sales   Fan clubs usually receive special access to tickets via ticket pre-sales.

farm team   A minor league baseball team that is owned by a major league team. Farm teams are used to develop talent.

Final Four   The last four teams in the NCAA (National Collegiate Athletic Association) basketball tournament. The term applies to both the men's and women's divisions.

floor seats   Seats located on the bottom floor of a venue.

franchise   A team; the legal framework that establishes ownership of a team.

franchise player   A star player around whom an entire franchise is built.

free agent   A player whose contract with his or her most recent team has expired, allowing him or her the freedom to sign a new contract with any offering team.

freebies   Free gifts given to fans for promotional purposes.

fulfillment   When the promises made to a sponsor by an organization or property in its proposal are kept and the sponsor realizes their return on investment.

garbage   Very bad seats.

general admission show   An event, typically a concert, where there are no assigned seats. (Formerly known as festival seating.) Sports stadiums will sometimes be leased out for such events.

gold circle seats A term used by some venues for their premium seats.

grassroot event Low cost sports competition conceived by a host organization for the purpose of attracting visitors into their community.

handling fee A fee added to the face value price of a ticket.

hard ticket A physical, printed ticket.

heating up The rising of ticket prices due to an event's popularity.

home team A term referring to the team on whose field, rink, or court the game is played. If the game is played on neutral grounds, the home team shall be designated by mutual agreement.

hospitality (or client/VIP entertainment) The hosting of key customers, clients, government officials, employees, celebrities, and other VIPs at an event. Typically includes tickets, parking, dining, and/or other amenities, often in a specially designated area.

host organization Sports commissions, convention and visitors bureaus, park and recreation departments, venues, and any other organization that hosts sporting events.

image advertising Advertising a product based on its association with an athlete or franchise, such as selling a type of sports drink by saying a star basketball player drinks it.

IP rights Intellectual property rights conferred by sponsorship (*See* licensing)

in-focus coverage The total amount of time the sponsor's marks or logos are visible to the viewing public during an event broadcast or news segment.

in-hand Tickets ready to be sold.

Everyone Knows

Stadium Subsidies

Over the past decade, one of the most heated debates in the sports world has centered around the notion of local economic stimulation through construction of tax-subsidized stadiums. Proponents of the plans point to short- and long-term job creation and to the myriad benefits of improved infrastructure, while critics typically blast the idea of helping millionaire owners and athletes get richer on the backs of the taxpayers.

in-kind sponsorship   Payment (full or partial) of sponsorship fee in goods or services rather than cash.

in-stock   Tickets ready to be sold.

insourcing   A continuing business service provided to a franchise by an outside organization, such as a catering company hired by a sports stadium to oversee concessions. It is different from "outsourcing" in that the client moves into or near the headquarters of the hiring organization.

intangible sponsorship benefit   A benefit whose value is based on its importance or uniqueness to the sponsor, i.e., exclusivity, prestige, audience makeup, etc.

interactive events   Pre-show clinics and tradeshows, to touch and feel events, games, and demonstrations.

inventory   All of the assets of an organization, property, or event are known as its inventory.

junk seats   Bad seats in a venue.

last minute transaction (LMT)   Buying a ticket so close to the date of the event that's there no time to mail the tickets. Instead, the purchaser must pick up the tickets at the will-call window at the venue.

licensing   The right to use a property's, event's, or agency's marks, slogans, or terminology in order to market or promote a sponsor's affiliation.

livery   Sponsor identification on racing cars, rally cars, support vehicles, etc. Livery design is a highly specialized art and all designs are generally camera-tested before approval.

local organizing committee (LOC)   Group of individuals in the community who form an ad hoc committee for the purpose of managing the procurement and running of sports events.

local pick-up   Tickets that are picked up at the venue.

lockout   Situation where a sponsor is able to prevent competitors from appearing or selling or promoting product at the same venue as the sponsor.

logo   The picture or image most closely associated with a sports team.

luxury box   An exclusive area at a sporting venue that offers a particularly great view of the event. Luxury boxes, also known as luxury suites, are often catered and are always very expensive.

market value   The price customers are willing to pay for tickets. This price is often much higher than the face value price.

media equitability   Accounting for and valuing media coverage or exposure received and comparing that to what you might have paid for the same coverage/exposure based on an appropriate and current media rate card.

media equivalencies   Measuring the exposure value of a sponsorship by adding up all the coverage it generated and calculating what it would have cost to buy a similar amount of ad time or space in those outlets based on media rate cards.

media sponsor   TV and radio stations, print media, and outdoor advertising companies that provide cash or, more frequently, advertising time or space, to a property in exchange for official designation.

merchandising   Any marketing method used to foster sales or audience growth.

mezzanine   The lowest balcony in a theater.

MVP   Most Valuable Player, an award given to the top athlete of a particular sports league every year.

NATB   National Association of Ticket Brokers.

naming rights   The naming of a facility or project as a catalyst to executing a specific marketing plan and presence.

narrowcasting   Using a broadcast medium to appeal to audiences with special interests. For example, an all golf channel would be a narrowcast, because it appeals to an audience with a specific interest.

national governing body (NGB)   Any sport organization responsible for rules and regulations of one or several sport activities. Usually membership-based and comprised of athletes, coaches, officials, and a national staff dedicated to the promotion and growth of the sport through city, state, region, or national level participation.

National Collegiate Athletic Association (NCAA)   A voluntary organization through which the nation's colleges and universities govern their athletics programs. It is comprised of institutions, conferences, organizations, and individuals committed to the best interests, education, and athletics participation of student-athletes.

niche marketing   The pursuit of a specific demographic or market territory instead of a mass market.

no oddlot   Refers to a portion of tickets that must be sold in even numbers.

no splits   A collection of tickets that must be sold and purchased as a group.

nosebleeds   Nickname for seats at a sporting venue that are the farthest away from the stage or the action. Name is derived from tendency of mountain climbers to get nosebleeds at higher altitudes.

obstructed view   Seats at a venue whose view of the event is obscured. Typically a pole or a camera is blocking a ticketholder's view.

official supplier   Provider of goods or services in exchange for designated recognition.

on-site pickup   Tickets that must be picked up at the venue hosting the event.

option to renew   Contractual right to renew a sponsorship based on specific terms.

overtime   A basketball, football, or hockey term referring to an extra period played to break a tie score at the end of a regulation game.

parking pass   A pass that enables its holder to park very close to the venue, usually in some sort of structure.

perimeter advertising   Stationary advertising around the perimeter of an arena or event site, often reserved for sponsors.

personal seat license (PSL)   A certificate of ownership for seats in a venue. However, even with a PSL you still have to buy tickets to a particular event.

philanthropy   Support for a non-profit or charitable property where no commercial advantage is expected.

piggyback seats   Tickets in two or more adjoining rows that have the same seat number. Instead of sitting next to someone, you're sitting behind or in front of them.

platform   The foundation for a successful sports sponsorship.

pre-sale   The sale of tickets to an event prior to when they are available to the general public. Pre-sale tickets are usually reserved for fan club members or other special groups.

premiums   Souvenir merchandise, produced to promote a sponsor's involvement with a property, usually customized with the names/logos of the sponsor and the property.

premium tickets   The best seats for an event.

presenting sponsor   The sponsor that has its name presented just below that of the sponsored property, i.e., "The Rose Bowl presented by Citibank."

Keeping
in Touch

Maintaining Contacts

With the advent of social media sites such as Facebook and LinkedIn, it has become imperative for professionals in all fields to maintain relations with former colleagues as well as develop new ones. Contacts from previous jobs can provide leads for new positions, provide references, and offer necessary counsel. Also, if you are thinking of changing positions (from marketing promotions assistant to marketing director, for instance), a call to an old boss could yield a great deal of information as to what the new job might entail. In short, keeping an open dialogue with past associates can be a wonderful way not only to locate new opportunities, but also to increase one's professional knowledge.

primary sponsor   The sponsor paying the largest fee and, therefore, receiving the most prominent identification.

primary ticket market   The original distributor of tickets to a particular event (usually Ticketmaster).

promoter   The organizer of an event. The promoter coordinates all details with the performer(s) and the box office.

property   Another term for the assets owned by an organization with the potential to be exploited by a commercial sponsor. The property may refer to a building, such as an arena or stadium, but it may also refer to an event.

proposal   The document that the owners of a property prepare to solicit a sponsorship from a corporation. The proposal will usually detail the inventory of assets, offer to bundle those assets, set the price for the bundle, and describe the process used to determine the price. It will also describe past events, the potential for activation, and other potential benefits to the sponsor.

prospect   The potential buyer of a sponsorship, typically a company who sells products thought to be of interest to the people interested in a certain property or event. Usually these prospects for sponsorships are consumer goods companies.

psychographics A term that portrays consumers or a targeted group based on psychological characteristics. These are determined by segmentation-produced tests which can be associated with product usage for predictive purposes.

public sector sponsorship Strategy linking a company to a community service, activity, venue, program, or event in the public domain (e.g., parks and recreation, schools, cities, municipalities, etc.).

rainout insurance For weather-sensitive events, ticket holders can purchase insurance on the chance that the weather forces a cancelation.

red shirt A designation given to a college player who is forced to sit out during a particular season due to injury, academic reasons, or the decision of the coach.

reserved seating A performance or event where every ticket corresponds to a specific seat.

response function Anticipated response to an advertisement or a campaign. Typically a generalization, but can refer to a mathematical formula relating investment to return.

return on investment (ROI) The method a sponsor uses to determine the business result from the sponsorship investment. There are various methods of determining ROI, depending on the sponsors' objectives. ROI may be very specific, such as the actual product sales at an event, or it may be more general, such as perceived increase in brand awareness over a given period of time.

right of first refusal Contractual right granting a sponsor the right to match any offer the property receives during a specific period of time in the sponsor's product category. Such rights are normally negotiated as part of an initial agreement.

rookie An athlete in the first year of his or her professional career.

scalper A derogatory term for someone who resells a ticket, typically outside the venue shortly before the event starts and for a highly-inflated price.

secondary ticket market Ticket resellers and the apparatus they use to sell tickets to fans.

segmented marketing The process of marketing to a particular market segment, demographic group, etc.

self liquidation The process of liquidating or subsidizing a sponsor's fee by passing the costs on to a third party. For example, a retailer commits to a sponsorship and then presents the opportunity to ten product vendors in exchange for financial support for the sponsorship.

selling air   The act of selling tickets not owned by the seller.

semiotics   The theoretical process exploring how individuals glean meaning from words, sounds, and pictures. Occasionally used in researching names for various products and services.

service charge   A fee added to the price of a ticket.

session   A designated timeframe of a larger event. Often applies to baseball double headers where a venue has both an afternoon and evening session. The venue is emptied in between sessions and admission into each session requires a separate ticket.

signage   Banners, billboards, electronic displays, etc. found in the arena that feature the sponsor's identification or message.

single   One ticket.

spoilage   Tickets that go unsold for an event.

sole sponsor   A company that has paid to be the only sponsor of a property to the exclusion of all others, although key trade sponsors are usually tolerated.

sponsor   An entity that pays a property for the right to promote itself and its products or services in association with the property.

sponsor ID   Visual and audio recognition of sponsor, e.g., sponsor name/logo on participant clothing, equipment, on property's publications and advertising, or via public-address and on-air broadcast mentions.

sponsee   A property available for sponsorship.

sponsorship   The relationship between a sponsor and a property, in which the sponsor pays a cash or in-kind fee in return for access to the exploitable commercial potential associated with the property.

sponsorship agency   A firm which specializes in advising on, managing, brokering, or organizing sponsored properties. The agency may be employed by either the sponsor or the property, and sometimes by both.

sponsorship fee   Payment made by a sponsor to a property.

sports commission   Organization created to support the creation and hosting of amateur sporting events in their community. May be born out of a chamber of commerce or convention and visitors bureau or be a department within a bureau.

sports event travel industry   Niche of the tourism industry that uses the hosting of sporting events to attract visitors to communities in order to drive economic impact.

sports marketing   Promotional strategy linking a company to sports (sponsorship of competitions, teams, leagues, etc.).

squatters   Event-goers that sit in seats not assigned to them.

SRO   Standing Room Only. Ticket holders must stand throughout the entire performance.

stay to play   Rule used by some events which requires participants to utilize certain hotels in order to be eligible to participate in competition.

strip   A series of tickets.

supplier   Hotels, sports publications, insurance companies, consulting and research firms, housing services, and any other company that supplies products and services to the sports event industry.

supplier sponsor   Status given for providing goods and services. Usually located below official sponsor status. *See* official supplier.

tangible sponsorship benefit   A benefit that is valued based upon its price or cost, such as media, signage, programs, venue rents, and so on.

ticket book   A group of tickets bound together like a book.

ticket broker   A legal reseller of tickets.

ticket hustler   Another name for a scalper.

ticket marketplace   Any location that allows ticket sellers and ticket buyers to interact and conduct business.

ticket scanner   A device used by event staff to electronically read your ticket's barcode.

ticket stub   The portion of your ticket returned to you after the event staff tears it.

Ticketmaster   The leading primary ticket seller in the United States.

title sponsor   The sponsor that has its name incorporated into the name of the sponsored property, e.g., Team Watson's, Gold Leaf Team Lotus.

usage and attitude (U&A) study   Research study that incorporates factors such as product purchase, usage, attitudes and awareness, and may also incorporate media exposure data.

underwriting sponsor   Typically backs a show or event with a line of credit in exchange for a sponsorship or equity position. Typically the sponsor is only tapped if the activity loses money.

uniforms   A vitally important ingredient in presenting a properly coordinated sponsorship image and message.

United States Olympic Committee (USOC)   Nonprofit organization recognized by the International Olympic Committee as the sole entity in the United States whose mission involves training, entering, and underwriting the full expenses for the U.S. teams in the Olympic, Paralympic, Pan American, and Parapan American Games. The USOC oversees the process by which U.S. cities seek to be selected as a candidate city to host the Olympic and Paralympic Games, winter or summer, or the Pan American Games. In addition, the USOC approves the U.S. trial sites for the Olympic, Paralympic, and Pan American Games team selections.

value proposition   What a franchise promises a sponsor (e.g., brand exposure, marketing space, improved branding) in exchange for sponsorship.

venue marketing   Promotional strategy linking a sponsor to a physical site (sponsorship of stadiums, arenas, auditoriums, amphitheatres, racetracks, fairgrounds, etc.). Such marketing typically includes signage, sampling, and other services as part of a package of benefits.

violation   A basketball term referring to an infringement of the rules that is not a foul. The penalty for a violation is the awarding of the ball to the opponent.

walk   An area near a venue where scalpers gather to sell tickets.

wall bangers   Seats located next to a wall, usually far away from the venue's prime seating.

wave machine   Type of poster site in which the whole display is changed at regular short intervals by rotation of (usually vertical) slats, to which different advertisements (usually for different products) are applied. Variations in banner format are now found frequently at sports venues.

will call   A clearly defined area of a venue, typically near the box office, where patrons can retrieve pre-ordered tickets.

Chapter 6

Resources

Now that you have read through this guide, you have acquired a strong working knowledge of the professional sports industry. As with any field, however, there is always more to learn. The additional resources collected here will point you in the right direction to discover more about this exciting field for yourself. These resources include associations and organizations, books, Web sites, and degree-granting programs.

Associations and Organizations

In many industries, joining a professional association or organization is essential (and sometimes even required). Membership in a group such as this can be beneficial in many ways. But primarily, it is helpful for networking purposes. You've probably heard the expression, "It's not what you know, it's who you know." This maxim remains as true as ever, and so it can never hurt to form a personal bond with members of the industry. The following associations and organizations provide invaluable contacts and information for industry insiders and newcomers alike.

The **American Marketing Association** The American Marketing Association (AMA) is the professional association for leaders in the practice, teaching, and expansion of worldwide marketing. There are some important roles that the American Marketing Association assist personnel in the field with. This agency

Problem
Solving

Case Study: Damage Control

Situation: While working in the public relations department of an NBA team, one of the players uses an unkind epithet to describe an opponent during a press conference after a particularly frustrating loss. You and the rest of the staff know he is a decent, good person, not prone to making such remarks. In the office the next morning everyone blames his slip on the fact that he scored a dismal seven points and that the game was the last in a grueling series away from home.

Problems: During the playing season, athletes are in the public eye as consistently as politicians, and the heat of a moment after an intense game may bring about unguarded behavior. The problem is that the general public does not take an individual's stress into account when evaluating his or her actions. A momentary loss of cool could have long-term ramifications for the player's image and marketing appeal, as well as the image of the team.

Solution: Your first step as a PR professional will be to meet with the team's executives and discuss how to get an angle on the story. Call on teammates to vouch for his personal integrity. Cite any examples of past volunteer work. Above all, afford the player an opportunity to apologize. Fans will appreciate a player who admits a mistake and apologizes honestly over one who attempts to justify an errant comment with farfetched excuses.

supports marketers to realize their full potential in their field. Support comes in the form of: continuing education, up-to-date market information and networking. Additionally, AMA provides a conduit for marketers to connect and share information with each other. Many job opportunities arise through the network of marketing professionals. Professional business and job opportunities are key resources from the AMA. The American Marketing Association also strives to provide information on the latest cutting-edge technology for marketing professionals, and best practices in the business. The AMA has provided and continues to provide industry information, educational opportunities, and marketing network opportunities that support marketers in their careers, boosting the overall standard of the industry. (http://www.marketingpower.com)

Association of Luxury Suite Directors The Association of Luxury Suite Directors was founded in 1990 with the goal of providing both teams and venues with accurate and timely data regarding the premium seating market in stadiums and arenas across North America. The organization is committed to gathering, supporting, and developing a network for individuals to share information, ideas, and values with one another in order to ensure profit and quality for all its members. Their ultimate goal is to assist members with providing premium seat patrons with excellent service, state-of-the-art amenities, and an overall outstanding experience. (http://www.alsd.com)

National Sport Marketing Network The National Sports Marketing Network (NSMN) is the most exclusive industry trade organization for sports business professionals within the United States. Founded in 1998, the NSMN includes nearly 9,000 individual and corporate members who re-join the organization on an annual basis. In addition to offering networking opportunities and educational programs, the NSMN organizes industry discounts and offers complimentary job matching services for its members. The organization includes both the leading newsmakers and leaders in the sports business industry, including but not limited to league commissioners, network executives, agency presidents, and corporate executives who organize and lead industry discussions. NSMN-produced programming has received national and local press coverage. NSMN is board-governed by sports business industry leadership. Membership is by application only, and applicants must have sports business work experience to qualify for membership. (http://www.sportsmarketingnetwork.com)

Sports Marketing Association The Sports Marketing Association (SMA) is an organization that works with sports marketing businesses as well as college and high school coaches and staff members. This association supports these two essential entities by providing industry information and education to players within the sports marketing business. The SMA tracks results in the industry and sends out the data to sports marketing firms, high schools, and universities. SMA also seeks to find solutions to the questions raised by the surveys they have executed. This agency uses its own publications, as well as others, to spread information throughout the industry. The SMA also sets up events where professionals in the marketing industry, students, coaches, and school staff can meet to discuss contemporary issues affecting all parties. One recent example of such an event was a panel discussion held at a major NBA basketball team's athletic center. This event offered students the opportunity to meet and discuss their careers with marketing professionals. Alumni were also invited to the event. The event culminated with a basketball game between two NBA teams. The SMA's ultimate goal is to include all members of the professional sport marketing community who seek to play a hand in future progression within the academic discipline and the field of sport marketing. (http://www.sportmarketingassociation.com)

Books and Periodicals

Seek out the following books and periodicals to expand your knowledge of the professional sports world.

Books

These books make an excellent addition to the library of any sports fan, especially one seeking employment in the industry.

Careers for Sports Nuts & Other Athletic Types. By William Ray Heitzmann (McGraw-Hill, 1997). This is a very useful informational book. It describes in detail occupations in the sports industry and athletic departments such as physical therapy, coaching, sports communications, and many more. This book is particularly useful for high school students who are looking to break into the sports industry.

Career Opportunities in the Sports Industry By Shelly Field (Ferguson Publishing Company, 2010). This book describes, in minute detail, the specific process by which one goes about starting a career (or changing one's current direction) in the sports industry. Seventy-three careers are described in an unambiguous and easy-to-understand style. The book also features boxed highlights of the facts in brief as well as a two-to-three page summary of each occupation, including the salary, employment prospects, educational requirements, and tips for entry. Finally, Ms. Field also provides lists of colleges, workshops, and professional associations.

The Comprehensive Guide to Careers in Sports. By Glenn M. Wong (Jones & Bartlett, 2008). This book offers an overview of what students should consider and expect from the various career choices available to them. It anticipates the questions students are most likely to ask, including which courses they should take, what specific areas are available to them, what their salary expectations should be, and how they can pursue the job of their dreams. In the highly competitive sports industry, it is crucial for individuals to prepare themselves well and to make the right decisions along the way. And while there are certainly no guarantees, this book can enhance a student's chances for success within the sports industry. Encouraging diligent research and realistic expectations, this book is the brainchild of an author with many years of experience as a respected practitioner, teacher, and internship coordinator.

The Dream Job: Sports Publicity, Promotion and Marketing. By Melvin Helitzer (University Sports Press, 1999). This third edition of the best-selling text on sports media and marketing has been utilized by over 150 colleges, universities, and professional sports organizations. The book's 18 chapters detail the responsibilities

Best
Practice

Interview Preparation

When preparing for an interview, people often spend so much time fine-tuning their résumés and honing their answers to an interviewer's potential questions that they neglect to adequately familiarize themselves with the organization to which they are applying. In the field of professional sports, a working knowledge of a team's history, strengths, and place in the marketing landscape can go a long way in impressing a potential employer. Candidates do not have to immerse themselves in the trivia of the team, but it is good to do a bit of research before the interview. It lets the interviewer know you want to be part of a team environment; what's more, it signals that you will be amenable to learning the team's methods and practices, and are committed to helping it succeed.

of a professional sports PR or college sports information director and offer insights on media writing, sports photography, broadcast interviewing, press conferences, statistics, creating new sporting events, promotion and marketing, crisis management and creating a Web page. *PR Week* magazine acclaimed the newest edition of the book as the best in the industry.

Periodicals

Stay in the loop with the latest professional sports news by reading these publications. Whether they are issued daily, weekly, or monthly, they will be invaluable as you begin to negotiate the industry.

ESPN the Magazine is the print counterpart to the very popular television network of the same name. Its bold graphics, photo-driven layout, and quality writing make it a well-respected publication by professionals and fans alike. The "Insider" feature on the Web site allows visitors to customize their news feeds to focus on their favorite teams and athletes, which is helpful if you are pursing a job in a particular market and want to be up on the latest events. (http://insider.espn.go.com/insider/espn-the-magazine)

SportBusiness International features updates on media developments, branding, and events for the worldwide sports community. It is an excellent resource to track changes of ownership and television and broadcasting contracts. Keeping up with this periodical will give you an insider's view into the strategies and tactics of sports professionals. (http://www.sportbusiness.com)

Sporting News is a well-regarded periodical with an intense focus on statistics and predictions of athletic performance. Widely used by agents and others who track the growth and development of athletes, *Sporting News* is also coveted amongst the fantasy-league set for its detailed analysis of players' strengths and weaknesses. Its "Fanhouse" section is a great compendium of columnists' assessments of the sports world. (http://aol.sportingnews.com)

SportsBusiness Journal is a daily magazine that covers all aspects of the professional sports industry. It reports on developments at both the league and team level, follows construction and refurbishment of sports facilities, and provides listings of industry conferences and events. Reading "Opinions" section is a good way to see how owners, managers, and other professionals are conceiving of the future of the industry. (http://www.sportsbusinessdaily.com)

Sports Illustrated is *the* classic sports magazine. Read by industry professionals and casual fans alike, *SI* (as it is known amongst its fans) covers news and trends of all the major professional sports, as well as collegiate athletics. Its annual "Sportsman of the Year" award is a highly respected honor with true historical pedigree. (http://sportsillustrated.cnn.com)

Web Sites

The following Web sites contain troves of information about the sports industry, as well as general business practices and tips for finding employment.

About.com About.com is a unique online content Web site that links users and companies by providing advertising space to companies that want to capture a market that researches information online. About.com provides information on topics like healthcare, sports, parenting, and travel, among other things. These represent a few of the 70,000 topics that About.com features online. Companies buy advertising space on the information pages that are relevant to the topics consumers are researching. (http://www.about.com)

Athletic Scholarships Athletic Scholarships is a sports online recruiting service that links college athletes to coaches and colleges that have sports scholarship opportunities. This service helps college athletes navigate through the complex set of NCAA rules and with the recruiting process. They work with NCAA Division I, II, and NAIA level colleges. This service essentially builds a sports/academic résumé for athletes and distributes it across the country to coaches looking for athletes. The athlete pays for this service. In addition to the recruiting service, the Web site offers historical information, FAQs, and current news on college sports. (http://www.athleticscholarships.net/aboutme.htm)

The Business of Sports This Web site is a blog owned and operated by Russell Scibetti. Mr. Scibetti is an independent sales and marketing consultant currently doing business with two professional sports organizations. His Web site offers news, trends, and data on the business and industry of sports. The blog researches and reports on ticket sales, sports media, brand management, fan loyalty, corporate sponsorships, and sports finances. The blog also posts networking/job fair events in cities around the country that help both job seekers and sports organizations link up or find information they may be looking for. (http://www.thebusinessofsports.com)

Fantasy Sports Ventures FSV is an online resource for news, historical information and gaming for fantasy sports, college sports, baseball, hockey, and football. FSV has over 15 million online subscribers/users. This Web site also uses about 600 online sports affiliates to service its users/members. FSV also provides advertising space to large companies like Sprint, McDonald's, Coca Cola, Coors, and Sprint Mobile that targets the online user market. (http://www.fantasysportsventures.com)

Forbes.com Forbes, Inc., is a giant publishing firm that specializes in financial and business news with regards to all industries worldwide, including the sports industry. Forbes, Inc., is best known for publishing its yearly Fortune 500 companies list in its magazine. (http://www.forbes.com)

HickokSports.com Ralph Hickok is a journalist who has written several books on American Sports: *Who Was Who in American Sports* (Hawthorne Books, 1971); *The New Encyclopedia of Sports* (McGraw-Hill, 1977); *The Encyclopedia of North American Sports History* and *The Pro Football Fan's Companion* (Macmillan, 1995); and *Who's Who of Sports Champions* (Houghton Mifflin, 1995). He currently keeps a Web site that offers historical and current data on a wide variety of sports. (http://www.hickoksports.com/whohick.shtml)

Jobs in Sports This site touts itself as "The Most Up-To-Date Sports Job Board. Period." It details opportunities at all levels within the professional sports, from internships to executive positions. Members have access to thousands of sports employment openings that are available today with industry leaders, professional organizations, and professional leagues and franchises. (http://www.jobsinsports.com)

Plunkett Research Ltd Plunkett Research, Ltd. was started in 1985. This online industry source provides industry analysis specifically regarding industry statistics and trends. Plunkett provides online subscriptions for industry experts (colleges, government agencies, and consultants). (http://www.plunkettresearch.com/Industries/Sports/SportsTrends)

TeamWork Online TeamWork Online "blends the best aspects of executive recruiters, job boards, applicant tracking systems, and online dating systems into the most advanced and integrated suite of recruiting tools and industry networks to help applicants find the right jobs and to help employers find the right candidates quickly and cost effectively." TeamWork Online's recruiting tools and industry networks increase the applicant's ability to find the right job quickly through numerous proven techniques, including digital matching tools (wherein each candidate is provided unique digital matching tools with employers to help him identify his most appropriate next job based on skill, location, salary, and sport), and the "Teammate" Network (which links candidates to potential colleagues and mentors based on common location, education, and work history). (http://www.teamworkonline.com)

Time Warner Cable Time Warner Inc. is a conglomerate of businesses that provide entertainment and news via television and publishing. Time Warner is the umbrella company for Turner Broadcasting System, Warner Brothers Entertainment, Home Box Office, and Time, Inc. Today Time Warner is one of the largest global media providers both online and on television. (http://www.timewarner.com/corp/newsroom)

Work in Sports Work In Sports is the number one job board and employment resource in the sports industry. It features hard-to-find sports jobs and internships nationwide. Resources include: résumé posting, career tips, job and internship postings, career spotlights from sports industry executives, and a directory of sports industry contacts. Work In Sports partnered with *Sports Illustrated* in 2001 to provide exclusive sports employment/career content for their official Web site, SI.com. (http://www.workinsports.com)

Educational Institutions

Associate's degree programs award students a two-year degree in sports management. If you are interested in entry-level work in marketing, administrative, or management work, you can pursue an associate's degree. As a two-year college student, you can expect to be taught how to use business practices and apply them to health, exercise, and nutrition. Most of these programs will require you to have a high school diploma or a general equivalency degree (GED). You will also have to submit your college testing scores from the SAT or ACT along with your high school transcript.

As a student in an associate's program, you will learn the fundamentals about human resources, finances, marketing, promotions,

Professional Ethics

Case Study: Recruiting Violations

Situation: You have been working as an assistant facilities manager at a college basketball stadium that plays host to one of the top programs in the country. When the facilities manager retires, the coach of the team recommends you for the position, as he has seen how hard you work and has come to know you in your tenure there. Since he is something of a legend on campus, the hiring board defers to his recommendation and selects you for the job. Now he wants something in return: a prized high school recruit is coming to visit the campus, and he asks you to set aside $500 worth of athletic equipment to pass along. He assures you it is not bribery and that coaches all across the country employ various means of lobbying top players.

Ethical Problem: Though the coach says otherwise, plying players with gifts or money in exchange for a commitment to play is clearly a recruiting violation. Other common violations include excessive phone calls to lobby players or the use of former players to recruit on behalf of their alma mater.

Solution: The coach may have helped you get your dream job, but being a part to his scheme could see you lose it just as fast as you were hired. Tell him that you are so thankful for the opportunity to work with such a storied program that you would do nothing to risk termination. Stand strong if he persists: college coaches of a certain stature are used to getting what they want, when they want, and do not take "no" for an answer. You should report his actions in confidence to the head of the athletic department, as most scandals of this nature become more problematic the longer they remain in the dark.

accounting, and operations. You will also take health and wellness science courses which focus on sports medicine and the biology of sports. Also included will be courses on topics such as sports counseling and psychology, rehabilitation of the athlete, and overall health and fitness.

With an associate's degree you will be fully equipped to find entry-level work with college teams, athletic associations, private fitness organizations (i.e., the YMCA or the Boys and Girls Clubs of America). You will work daily with athletes and other sports professionals such as agents and media personnel. Some of the jobs that are available to qualified individuals are: sports agent, sports manager, sports facility operator, athletic program director, public relations/media representative, or sports marketing specialist.

As a professional in the sports business, you will be expected to continue your education, network with colleagues in the business, and gain experience before you can earn higher wages. Many positions require sports administrators to gain experience before obtaining higher positions and salaries. You can join the North American Society for Sport Management (NASSM) to help further your career.

Getting a B.A. will help you to advance at a faster rate in the sports industry. You will be able to pick up management jobs much faster than with an associate's degree. Many B.A. degrees in sports management offer courses in collegiate sports management, coaching and athletic development, sports marketing, exercise science, and sports administration. You can expect to find work with professional sports teams, collegiate teams and private organizations. There are several universities that offer quality B.A. degrees in sports management. Below are a few that are spread across the United States. If you still need to read more on what college is right for you, check the Internet for Web sites that promote colleges with sports management programs, read blogs that specialize in sports management schools (for example, College Confidential), or visit your local library to get information. You can also call any of the colleges you find listed to have information sent to you.

Indiana University offers bachelor's, master's and doctoral degree programs in sports management. This university responded to the growing needs of the sports industry and began programs for three degrees in 1985. The focuses of the two- and four-year programs are sports management and marketing. However, the doctoral program prepares students to enter an academic setting. Indiana University also offers programs that can be combined with courses from their business school, Kelley School of Business. This further enhances a student's preparation in entrepreneurship and sports marketing and management. (http://www.indiana.edu)

North Carolina State University benefits from the excellent sports reputation of the geographic location as well as the quality college sports reputation. Students can be exposed to top sports-marketing executives and professionals. The bachelor's degree program focuses primarily on sports marketing, with courses in finance, sports journalism, and events marketing as part of the program. (http://www.ncsu.edu)

The **University of Florida** takes a unique approach to its sports management program by providing a combined bachelor of science and master of science degree in sports management. Students earn both degrees in five years instead of the typical six it takes to complete a traditional bachelor's and master's program. Courses that are offered include classes in law, finance, management leadership, ethics, and sports management. Students that choose to go to the University of Florida also benefit from having an advisor that helps them structure their program to meet their specific educational needs. (http://hhp.ufl.edu)

The **University of Massachusetts** offers a combined master of science in sports management and a master of business administration degree. Students do earn two degrees from this school. The Isenberg School of Management offers students a business-oriented program in sports management. Fulltime students can earn their dual degrees in two years. Courses are offered in sports licensing, sports marketing, broadcast communications (print and online), event management, management theory, and organization behavior theory. Students have the opportunity to partner with sports marketing companies and professional and collegiate sports organizations. (http://isenberg.umass.edu)

Index